EXT. 170

MY JOURNEY OF
SACRIFICE, HEARTBREAK, AND TRIUMPH
FROM STOCKER TO STORE MANAGER!

KEVIN L. GAINES

EXT. 170
My Journey of Sacrifice, Heartbreak, and Triumph from Stocker to Store Manager!

iUniverse books may be ordered through booksellers or by contacting:

iUniverse
1663 Liberty Drive
Bloomington, IN 47403
www.iuniverse.com
844-349-9409

ISBN: 978-1-6632-0562-9 (sc)
ISBN: 978-1-6632-0561-2 (e)

Library of Congress Control Number: 2020921445

Print information available on the last page.

iUniverse rev. date: 01/18/2021

This book is dedicated to my wife,
Keshia L. Gaines, PhD. Thank you for
always believing in me. I love you.

INTRODUCTION

Over half of millennials believe their lives should be made into a movie. Although I don't share that same sentiment, I do believe my career's journey is an interesting one. *Ext. 170* documents my journey through heartbreak and triumph. In my journey, I did not have a roadmap to success. I had to rely heavily on others for knowledge and for strength. During my darkest hour, I had to dig deep and keep going. There were times I wanted to give up, but I didn't. There were times when I should have quit, but I didn't. I was told no over forty times before someone finally said yes! From humble beginnings to my finest hour, join me as I take you through my journey, and enjoy!

Kevin L. Gaines

CHAPTER 1

The Beginning

I remember sitting there in my office and staring at the phone. I was in shock about what had just happened. As I gathered my thoughts, I realized that the commutes, the late nights, and all the sacrifices were worth it.

Let me start from the beginning. I grew up in a small town with a population of roughly five thousand people. One issue with small towns is lack of jobs. Once you were hired, you probably did not want to leave that job in that town. If you did, you may not get another. This posed a problem for young people like me. It was 1997, and I had just turned fifteen and was eager to get into the workforce. I started applying everywhere. I applied at almost every store in town that could legally hire a fifteen-year-old. I remember applying at three grocery stores, including Sunflower, Ramey's, and 84 Grocery. All of them were booked solid and were not hiring. They also had a ton of applications ahead of mine, so I knew my chances were slim to none.

This was the year I became an official high school student by entering the ninth grade. As I embarked on my new journey, I noticed a stark difference between some of those students and me. A lot of them seemed happy and would often brag about what they had. Although I was never too materialistic, it did make me a bit jealous. Hearing stories from other classmates about their lavish vacations on Christmas breaks and what they did last summer struck a nerve with me. I wanted to be able to tell stories like that, but I was in no position to do so.

I decided at the moment I was going to have that, and I was going to do it on my own. As my mother and I were headed home from a store one day, I noticed a new building was being renovated near Hubert Square. I asked my mom to drive by and see what it was. I noticed a sign on the door that said, "Now Hiring." I asked my mom if I could go speak to someone, and she gave me her blessing. As I approached the front door, I met a man named Kyle. He explained to me that they were renovating the building for a new grocery store, and the name would be Save-A-Lot. He told me he was hiring. He handed me a paper application and told me to bring it back the next day. As I was walking away, he called my name and said, "Don't worry about the application right now. Be back tomorrow, ready to work. We will finish your application then." I couldn't have been more excited. At that moment, everything was right in the world. I walked out to my mother's car calmly and got in. She asked me how it went. Unfortunately, I did not hear her because all I could hear was a rendition of Kool and the Gang's "Celebration"! When I did snap out of it, I told her I got the job, and we both rejoiced. I had done it—I had arrived! I was going to be working at this new grocery store, and finally I could get those lavish things my schoolmates spoke of! Little did I know this was the start of what would become a career in retail.

I still remember my first day, waking up and being nervous. I also remember stressing out over an exam that I hadn't quite studied for because of the excitement of the new job. Luckily, that exam was in calculus. I loved math, so I was able to get through the exam and pass with flying colors. After class, it was back to daydreaming about my new job. I also began thinking about how I was going to balance class, football, basketball, all the clubs I was a member of, and a job. Throughout the rest of the day, it felt like time had stopped and school was never going to be over! I felt like I should fake sick and call Mom to come get me. I also knew that was not how I was built, so I stayed.

When the bell rang, I was out of class faster than a cornerback could return an interception. I hopped on the bus, went home, got dressed, and then rode my bike to the store because it was not too far from my house. As I walked in, I was handed a red-collared shirt that had the company logo on it. It seemed like the shirt was handed to me in slow motion with the song "Hallelujah" playing in the background. Once I finally finished my application, it was time to get to work. The store was still being renovated, so there were no groceries, just an empty store full of fixtures and equipment. I was introduced to Billy, who was the store assistant manager. He told me he would be the one to guide me along as I began my new job. He showed me what needed to be done that day, which was building a few counters and a few other things. Once we finished, he said to me, "You really work fast." I told him it was just the way I was built; I put all I had into everything I did and was very competitive. I told him I didn't like to play second fiddle to anyone, and I strived to be the best worker he had ever seen.

As I wrapped up my day, Kyle came over and told me what a great day of work I had put in, adding I should be back tomorrow. This continued for about two weeks. I was working a lot of hours but did not realize how many until I got my first paycheck. I had worked every day, including longer hours on the weekends, so that first paycheck was really nice. I really enjoyed what I was doing, but there was a lot more to be done. Once the store was fully renovated, I knew it would be a success. The store was freshly painted and had brand-new fixtures, coolers, and registers. After two weeks, Kyle finally gave me a day off but also told me to be back on Monday evening ready to work and have some fun. Boy, was I grateful for that day off. Luckily, this was not during football or basketball season, so I was able to work the hours after school.

After class on Monday, I went to the store to get started for my shift. As I entered the store, I just saw an endless row of pallets filled with groceries and general merchandise. Kyle met me by the front door and told me, "Billy taught you how to build fixtures, but I am going to teach you how to be a stocker." He told me that in order for me to be successful, I would need a weapon. I was visibly startled until he handed me a four-inch piece of metal that looked like a slice of gum. He said it was small but was effective and would make my job much easier. As I slid the weapon out of the casing, I noticed the tip was sharp and then noticed it was a razor. Kyle then said, "Here is your weapon and key to success: a company-issued box cutter." I had not used a box cutter up to that point, so naturally I thought it was the coolest thing ever. Kyle showed me how to safely navigate a box cutter. He taught me how to open boxes, stock the product, and break down boxes in the most efficient way that he knew. He then showed me how to read barcodes and labels. He then asked me if I could do it on my own. I told him of course. He said, "All right, then. Here is your pallet. I will be back in an hour or so to check on you."

He came back, and I was not where he left me. He walked across the store, and I was working another pallet. He told me, "This is not where I told you to be."

I replied, "Yes, sir, but I finished that pallet thirty minutes ago, and instead of standing around and waiting on you, I found more work. I like to earn my paycheck."

Truly amazed by this aggressive attitude, Kyle quickly gave me more work—and more importantly, more hours. I gave everything I had to each and every case that I put on the shelves. I was so grateful to have a job and have my own money that I did not want to risk losing it. Within a few weeks, the store was clean, stocked, and well conditioned, as we called it. Everything came together smoothly. I had got to know new people and learned how to work hard, be self-sufficient, and develop a great sense of urgency. I also enjoyed the fact that I had met new people and developed new relationships. There was one familiar face whom I knew. She was two grades ahead of me, and we went to the same high school.

It was finally time for our store to open. Unfortunately, I could not attend because I was at school. Three o'clock couldn't come fast enough. I ran home, got dressed, and headed to work. When I walked in, there were a ton of people shopping everywhere. Our hard work had paid off. Our store was finally open, and I couldn't be happier.

CHAPTER 2

A New Routine

A few weeks after the store opened, I realized how hard it was to maintain going to school, being active in school clubs, being active in sports, and maintaining a job. I was an honor student and did not want my grades to be negatively affected by the job. Like always, I simply worked harder. For months, my life was routine. I woke up, went to school, went to work, got off, studied, slept about five hours, and did it all over again the next day. Then finally school was out for the summer! I couldn't have been more excited because it meant I could work more hours.

There was a small matter of getting in shape for football season, so I had a new routine. Each morning at 6:00 a.m., I would call one of my best friends, Dantel, and let him know that I was on my way to pick him up to work out. I had known him since we were kids, and he was like a brother to me. His nickname was Slue. By then, with the assistance of my mother, I had my own car. I always told him that I would be there in five minutes, so he should be ready. I could tell he was always going to go right back to sleep soon as we got off the phone, but I was fully prepared to wake him once I arrived. He had a job at another local grocery store, so he also understood the need to balance a job and school. Once I arrived at his house, I had to bang on the door rather hard because just as I predicted, he would always fall asleep again. I had no mobile phone, so I had to have the faith of Job that he would wake up. He did most days. Once I picked him up, we headed to pick up another friend. The same scenario applied to him and he was never awake, so I had to honk my horn quite a few times.

We then went to the weight room at War Eagle Fieldhouse. Every football player had to do a minimum of three workouts a week in order to get in shape for the football season. The weight room was open all day, but we had to go early because we had jobs. I was always the motivator of the group and the one who had to get the party started in the weight room. After we stretched, we mainly concentrated on legs and upper body through bench-pressing and squats. We also concentrated on explosion techniques through the use of jump boxes and several other pieces of equipment that were available. We had to be careful because if we were not, we could get hurt and would not be able to play. I remember very clearly an incident where I was about to go through a round on the jump boxes. I jumped on one, two, and three with no issues. When I got to number four, I slipped and fell. You would think that one of your best friends would come check on you to make sure you are okay, right? Well, unfortunately that wasn't the case. As I was on the floor reeling in pain, barely conscious, I looked over my head and saw Slue laughing to the point where he couldn't breathe! After about ten minutes of laughter, he finally helped me up. I eventually forgave him for that. My favorite part of our workout was when we were building our endurance through cardio. This involved running up and down the bleachers in the stadium and pulling tractor tires on the field. We did this for the entire summer.

It was soon time to start school again, and I had a huge decision to make. Although I loved my job, I knew that I loved participating in school activities a little more, especially football. I had started every game as a freshman. I was now a starter on our varsity team and was not about to give it up. I made the decision that I was going to have to quit my job so I could play football. We had practice every day during the week and games on Friday nights, so I would not be available to work many hours. Apparently someone had told Assistant Manager Billy that it was a possibility I would be leaving the store. He approached me and told me not to worry; I could simply work on weekends until football season was over. He told me I was the best worker he had ever seen, and he did not want to lose me. This was music to my ears, and I told him how much it meant that they were willing to work with me.

Each week I now had a new routine. I woke up, went to school, went to practice, took Slue home, and then went home to do homework and study. I had games on Friday nights and worked on Saturday mornings. Going to work on Saturday morning was tough because I was so beat up from Friday night's game. A few times I had swollen ankles and hurt ribs, but I powered through it and was able to finish my weekend shifts. At the end of the football season, I elected not to pursue basketball any longer and wanted to concentrate on football, my job, and my studies.

After that football season, Kyle and Billy called me into the office and told me they wanted to offer me an assistant manager position. They told me that I showed maturity beyond my years, and they had never seen a worker who was so focused and had as much will as I did about my job. They knew I was only sixteen years old at the time, but to them it did not matter. Kyle mentioned he had spoken with the owner. I gladly accepted. Now I once again had a new routine. I would wake up, go to school, and then go manage my store.

CHAPTER 3

Learning How to Manage

I never made becoming an assistant manager at a grocery store a goal, but there I was. After the initial shock and celebration with my mother, it was time to get to work. It didn't take much training for me to catch on. I was taught how to open and close the store. I was taught how to do daily accounting paperwork, including store deposits. I was even taught how to use the store's ordering system to get in product. One of the most difficult things that I encountered was trying to garner the respect of my peers and the rest of the employees at the store. Most of them were older than me or were current classmates of mine. There were numerous instances where I had disagreements over poor productivity and other performance opportunities. The phrase "I'm not going to kill myself for this job" was repeated to me more times than I could count. I wasn't asking people to kill themselves. I was asking the workers to give me everything they had every time, because this was the way I was built.

I learned very quickly that people are different. Some people want to be the best, but others do not. Some people want to lead and manage, but others do not. To some, hard work and earning money the right way is a priority, but to others it is not. At one point, it became increasingly difficult to get work priorities completed. Maybe I was too hard. Maybe I was too nice. Whatever the issue was, I had decided I would do it all myself. Instead of being an assistant manager, I turned myself into a super stocker. I was a machine. I stocked, conditioned, cleaned, gathered buggies, and still did the managerial duties that I was taught to do. I stopped asking employees to basically do anything except check out customers. I was the evening assistant manager during the week and the opening assistant manager during the weekend because I was still in high school. This meant my time spent with the other managers were limited; when I came in, they went home.

Apparently, my store manager had heard from an employee that everyone was taking advantage of my ability to get everything done on my own. He met with me and gave me a few pointers. He asked me if I thought he was a good manager. I told him of course. He then told me something I would never forget. He told me that he was only as good as his employees. He told me the art of managing involves getting work done through others and not doing it all yourself. Although I was being a super stocker, all my employees were standing around and doing only the minimum to secure their weekly paychecks. He told me in order to be a successful manager, I was going to have to hold the employees accountable for their tasks. If they could not get it done, then maybe they shouldn't be here. After I closed the store, I went home that night and thought about what Kyle had said. I knew he was right, and I knew I had to change my management style. I also knew that I was about to make a lot of my classmates angry.

After pondering for hours about how I was going to change the next day, I realized I had forgotten one important thing: homework! I had a big exam the next day and knew I needed to study, so I quickly switched from manager to student. I remember being extremely tired that night, and I started to fall asleep as I was studying. I closed the book and told myself I was going to take a quick ten-minute nap and then wake up and finish my studies. When I woke up, it was six o'clock in the morning. The exam was at 8:00 a.m., and I hadn't finished studying. While getting dressed, I continued to study as best I could. I had come to the realization that I was going to fail. It must have been my lucky day because as I arrived for class, I noticed there was a substitute teacher in the room. She said the regular teacher was out sick, so she was filling in. The substitute then mentioned we would not have the exam that day, and it would be postponed until the teacher returned. God was definitely watching over me and had my back like always!

When school was over that day, I rushed to work. I relinquished my role of super stocker and gave the employees on the evening shift all the work. I explained to them that every task had a specific name by it. I also explained that the store manager had a copy of it as well. If their tasks were not completed, then the store manager and I would need to schedule a meeting with those employees. Not only did the employees get their tasks done, but they got them done in record time. I was able to get my managerial duties completed without the added stress of everyone else's assignments. Some days were better than others, and it was not always perfect, but I no longer had to be super stocker. I could finally be what I was supposed to be: an assistant manager.

CHAPTER 4

A New Start

Throughout the remainder of high school, I learned and developed more than I could have imagined. I learned to be a good student, a good athlete, and an advocate for change in our community through good work, and I had learned the art of managing. By my senior year, I had decided that I wanted to be an accountant. I scored a 27 on my ACT and had been accepted into several renowned colleges and universities. In the year 2000, I made a decision that would change my life. During awards night my senior year, I received over twelve awards and scholarships. One of those scholarships included a leadership scholarship to the University of Southern Mississippi. Before I left the awards ceremony, l had decided that I was going to college with a purpose. It was a great school, and it was only an hour away from home. This was such an exciting time for not only me but my entire family. I was set to become the first person in my family to attend a university.

As I came in to my shift after school one day, the store manager asked me if I was quitting because I was attending school. By this time, there was a new store manager; Kyle had taken the same position with another company. I told him that I could work weekends only. I did not want to drive every day back and forth an hour, plus pursue a degree. I felt as though I would fail. The new store manager agreed. I remember thinking on graduation night that I had my entire life mapped out, and it was going to be easy. I had worked hard and stayed the course. I was in a great relationship, I had friends, I had received several scholarships to a university, I was assistant manager at a grocery store at such a young age, and I was becoming a man.

The transition to college was not as easy as I had anticipated. As I was preparing to go to college that summer, I worked as hard as I could and as many hours as I could to save money. During that summer, my relationship ended, so the transition became a little tougher. I was entering college with a heavy heart and felt alone. One of the prerequisites of my leadership scholarship was staying on campus. Luckily, my roommate was at least one familiar face. He had attended my high school and had been in my class. He decided to stay on campus as well.

It was finally move-in day, and it was a day I will never forget. My mother and a friend accompanied me and helped me move in. I will never forget the look on her face when it was time for her to leave. Holding back tears, she told me she loved me and how proud she was of me. She also told me that she was sad because I was leaving home, and she could no longer protect me. But she also told me she was not worried because God was always with me. She quoted scripture, said prayers for me, and gave me the biggest hug that she could. As she drove away, I took a deep breath and then proceeded to my dorm room.

I was excited to be on my own for the first time, but I was nervous. My hometown's population was only five thousand people, so to be in a school with over thirteen thousand and a city over forty-two thousand was a little overwhelming. After my roommate and I set up our room, we explored our new city. We wanted to see what a college town looked like. One stark difference I noticed was the heavy amount of traffic and how fast people were driving! I was used to going thirty or forty miles per hour all the time. Everyone seemed to be in a rush while driving there. As we explored, I took in all what my new city had to offer. This included multiple entertainment venues and plenty of recreational opportunities. We stopped by a few stores and picked up a few things for our dorm room. Once we got back on campus and set up our room, I called my mother from the phone in our room, reassured her I was fine, and told her not to worry. Class was tomorrow, and I was eager to get to work on my degree.

I woke up early the next morning because it had been tough to sleep the night before. I was not used to being away from my family, so my night was filled with constant tossing and turning. I decided I was going to get dressed early and find the building where my first class was held. My schedule was full on Mondays, Wednesdays, and Fridays. My classes ended at 11:15 a.m. on Tuesdays and Thursdays. I walked across campus and found out there were a few more familiar faces from my graduating class. This was great news because I knew I wasn't alone.

I was pursuing a degree in accounting, but part of my curriculum during my freshman year was to take a few basic courses, including American History. Coincidentally, one of my favorite subjects in high school was my very first class in college. I arrived at Bolton Hall and found my room. I was expecting a classroom style setting, but this was not the case. I didn't enter a room—I entered an auditorium. There had to be at least two hundred seats in this room. I was one of the first to arrive, so I decided to meet the instructor. After we exchanged pleasantries, the class began to fill in. I thought to myself,

This is really happening. I'm about to begin my official first day of class! I was ready and thought it would be a breeze. *It is history. How hard could it be?* Oh my God! From the time he handed us the syllabus to the time class was over, I was in total shock. This was nothing like high school. It was hard, I was going to fail, and I was going to get kicked out of school for making the lowest grade of all time. I proceeded to my next class, and it was more of the same. This happened all week long, and I could not wait until Friday was over. I felt suffocated all week, but I knew I would be able to breathe after the week was over. I was wrong. Late Friday night, I remembered I needed to be back in my hometown to go to work Saturday morning. It was an hour drive, so I packed my clothes and drove home for the weekend. My first official week in college was over, but now I had to get back to work.

CHAPTER 5

A New Job

I returned to work Saturday morning ready to give my all, but I couldn't. I couldn't focus like I had before. I did not have that fire and desire to give everything I could. I couldn't pull it together, and it showed. The employees were unfocused during my shift and decided to horseplay and not get their tasks done. They had decided they were not going to do what needed to be done and couldn't care less about the consequences. What was even more disturbing was that I allowed it to happen. This continued for a month. Every weekend I came home, it was more of the same. I had become so focused on my class schedule that I had lost my way. I had lost the ability to bring out the best in people and had lost my ability to manage effectively.

In early September 2000, I was called to the backroom to meet with the store manager and the other assistant manager. I was informed that I was being demoted back to a stocker. He said the owner was no longer impressed with my work, and I was too young to hold an assistant manager position anyway. Needless to say, I was very angry. I knew there was no one in that building who worked harder than me. I knew no one cared about that store more than I did. I was angry that the store manager did nothing to help me. He did not try to help me find my way back to being the manager I once was. Sadly, as I handed over the keys, he told me that I could continue to work, but as a stocker on the weekends. I said I understood and walked away. My anger quickly turned into disappointment. I was disappointed I had allowed it to happen. I was heartbroken, was still trying to adjust to college life away from home, and had just gotten demoted from a position I had worked hard to get. Life at that moment had truly given me lemons.

When I returned to college the following Monday, I knew I had to get my act together before things got worse. I spoke with my mother, and she advised me to seek employment near the university so I would not have to drive on weekends to go to work. This would allow me to focus on school more and focus on my job at the same time. I took her advice and began seeking employment. For a week, I applied everywhere I could. I applied at the local post office, a few lumber companies, and several retailers. I finally secured a job at a Piggly Wiggly grocery store as an overnight stocker. This was great because it was only ten miles from the university. Working overnight would allow me to focus on my studies during the day. The following day, I drove home, turned in my notice, and informed the store manager that I would be leaving in two weeks.

Once I worked out my notice, I began my new job. I was working from 10:00 p.m. to 6:00 a.m. five nights a week. I was able to focus more on my studies without having to drive home every weekend. I did not need much training because I had three years of prior experience working in a grocery store. However, I learned that Piggly Wiggly did things a little differently than what I was accustomed to, so I needed to adapt. I worked with a team of five men overnight. At my previous job, we simply worked the merchandise off of the pallet

17

and stocked it to the shelves. At Piggly Wiggly, they used a technique called spotting. This technique meant they brought all the pallets to the floor, removed every case from the pallet, and placed it on the floor down the aisle where it was to be stocked.

At first I thought this was not going to be efficient. As my first night commenced, I began to have doubts. Once we finished spotting, I looked down the aisles, all I could see was a mound of groceries thrown on the floor that looked like the Great Wall of China. We picked up all the empty pallets, swept the floors, and then cleaned the backroom. Two hours into my shift, I had yet to stock a single case of merchandise. All I could think was, *I am not going to get finished, and I am going to lose my job the first night.* The manager in charge assigned me to the soup aisle and the canned vegetable aisle. He handed me a box cutter and said, "Get after it." I told him no worries because this was what I did!

I began cutting cases and putting merchandise on the shelves like my life depended on it. Case after case, the mound of merchandise on my aisles began to disappear. I knew I had to be going faster than anyone on the Piggly Wiggly roster. As I finished my aisles, I heard that same familiar sound on the aisles next to me. I heard that sweet sound of a razor tearing into cases and merchandise going on the shelves as quickly as possible. I stopped for a moment and took a peek down other aisles to see how the other stockers were doing. All the other stockers were finishing up their aisles just as I was. Their aisles were neat, clean, and well conditioned, as was mine. At that moment, I realized I was not the fastest stocker alive. I realized I was working with people with experience, and they knew what they were doing. I was relieved that I was not going to have to do additional work because the other workers couldn't finish, like at my previous job. I also grew a little jealous as well. No one was supposed to be able to outstock me!

Where did these people come from? I was excited at the same time because we all hit it off and developed great relationships. However, I was not going to allow what had happened that night to happen again. No one on that overnight crew was going to outstock me.

After I got off the next morning, I quickly rushed to my dorm room, showered, and got dressed for Economics class at 8:00 a.m. I always sat as close as I could to the front of the class so I could see and hear. This was one of my favorite courses, so I was always fully engaged, answered questions when I could, and did assignments for extra credit. As the professor discussed gross domestic product, I suddenly felt my eyes getting heavy. In the front row of class, in front of everyone, I went to sleep. Apparently I was snoring, and my head leaned back. The professor called my name, and my head snapped back faster than a Tyson knockout. I didn't know what had happened, but I quickly got myself together and began paying attention again, to no avail. I kept falling asleep. I was tired, and my body was letting me know it. I was so tired that I fell asleep in every class that day. Once class was over at three, I rushed back to my dorm room to take a nap before I had to be back at work the next night.

I also needed to study and do my homework. This was going to be a lot harder than I had expected! I had to be at work at 10:00 p.m., so I set my alarm to wake me at 8:00. I must have been very tired because I missed my wake-up call. When I finally woke from the deepest sleep in my life, it was 9:00. It took twenty minutes to get to work, so I quickly got dressed and started on my way. While driving, I realized that I had not done any of my course work that was due the next day. That was okay because I knew I had a lunch break; I would simply do it then. My mentality then shifted back to the true task at hand. I knew that I had to do my job better and faster than everyone that night. I knew that there was no way anyone working on that overnight crew was going to outstock me. I simply wasn't going to let it happen.

When I entered the store, all I could here in my mind was the song "King of the Jungle." I entered the store with such a fierce attitude that others noticed it the moment I clocked in. I was so focused that I almost missed the kickoff meeting that began each shift because I went straight to work. Once we got all the pallets down stacked on the aisles, my box cutter began its initial descent so deep into one of the boxes that I almost cut through all the product. I knew after the first few cases this night was mine. I was focused, had a good rhythm, and had more energy than anyone there. I kept at it for four hours straight. Midway through my shift, I was done with my assigned aisles. All merchandise was worked to the counter, my aisles were straightened, and they were clean. I took a peek at the other workers' aisles, and they weren't even close. Of course, the manager told me good job, but he also told me to go help someone else. I was new and so didn't argue. When lunchtime arrived, I went to my car, turned on a light, and began my homework.

As I started, my eyes got heavy, and I fell asleep. When I woke up, it was time to return to work. I went back into the store but wasn't focused on work. I was worried about how I would get the assignments done before class. The manager could tell I was not the same person I was before lunch because my productivity went down substantially. He asked me what was wrong, and I simply told him I would do better. I never have been an excuse-driven person, and I was not about to let it be known I was secretly very stressed inside. I tried to be the best at work and be the best in class. Long story short, I didn't. My first class was at 8:00 a.m., and I did not get off until 7:00. It took me twenty minutes to drive back to campus. I got dressed and then headed to class. The first thing the professor did was whip out a pop quiz from last night's reading assignment. Needless to say, I didn't fare too well. The standard 17 percent curve that he issued on most graded assignments still didn't help. He graded them on the spot, and I was sure I had the lowest grade in the class. People were giving each other high-fives and accolades. My neighbor asked me about my grade after class, and I somehow got off the subject and began talking about the collapse of Enron or anything else I could think of.

I walked away from that class tired and defeated. As a matter of fact, every class that I took that day became a joke. I couldn't focus, I was falling asleep, and I was already failing. I was so disappointed in myself because my body was failing me and wouldn't allow me to do as much as my brain wanted to do. I had to fix it. I knew if I continued like this, I wasn't going to make it past my first semester in college. I went to the registrar's office to try to change my class schedule so they would begin later in the day. Unfortunately, I could not because all the courses I wanted were already full. Disappointment set in again.

After the week was over, I went home to my mother's house. I was off from work that weekend, so it was a perfect time to detox and develop a new plan. I sat in my room and tried to figure out what to do next. I then fell to my knees, prayed, asked for guidance, and asked for strength. One of the things that I had relied on my entire life up until that point was sheer will. I was always the hardest worker and the most intense person in the room. I wouldn't allow anything to defeat me, and if it did, I considered it a minor setback. That was what allowed me to be an honor student and good athlete in high school. This was also what made me want to be the best at everything I did. I didn't like losing and enjoyed being number one. At that moment, I decided that I was simply going to power through it. I was going to use my sheer will to get through my first semester of college no matter what. I looked in the mirror and said to myself, "Let's do this thing."

CHAPTER 6

Semester Two

Throughout my first semester, I faced a litany of challenges that included fatigue, anxiety, and a sense of failure. Semester one was coming to an end, so I took a moment to reflect on what I had accomplished. I was the first in my family to attend a university, I had gotten a new job, and I had finally established a routine that would help me make it through each day. I also was getting very little sleep, I lost contact with most of my friends, and I was failing in class. I had to make a change. I was doing exactly what I said I would not do: fail. By that point, I had gotten a promotion managing the overnight crew at my job, but I felt empty. I was winning at work but losing in college.

As the new semester began in January, it was more of the same. The semester began with my falling asleep in class after a tough night at work, missing assignments, and failing tests. I became increasingly disappointed in myself that it briefly made me want to drop out of school. That was not how I was built, though. I wasn't dropping out, and I certainly wasn't going to accept failure. When February came around, I was in desperate need of a change and needed help. I remember walking into Nutrition class, sitting there, and wondering why I had to take Nutrition. What did nutrition have to do with getting an accounting degree? I also sat there trying to figure out what to do next. I was then tapped on the shoulder by a young lady named Keshia, who asked me for a sheet of paper. When I turned around and gazed in her eyes, it was like seeing an angel. I was a bit shy, so after passing her the sheet of paper, I did not say much. She, on the other hand, had an outgoing personality and tried to get to know me through conversation. I said a few words but was not able to connect like I wanted to. When class ended, we exchanged a few more words but failed to exchange phone numbers, which was what I really wanted. I had missed out on a golden opportunity to make a new friend—or perhaps something more. What if I never saw her around campus? Would I see her next week? What if she dropped the course, and I didn't see her again? I was disappointed in myself yet again. What was I doing?

A week went by, and I was still falling asleep in class, I was still not getting any sleep, and I still was failing. It was time for Nutrition class again. I hoped I would see that angel from the week before, but I did not. I was disappointed. About ten minutes into class, she finally walked in. She was running late apparently. I couldn't have been happier. She sat right in front of me and gave me one of those flirty looks. At that moment, I knew I was making my move. She was not getting out of class without me getting her phone number. When class ended, I walked her to the commons area, which was universally known as the cafeteria. I asked her for her number, and she would not give it to me but instead took mine. I didn't have a mobile phone, so I gave her my dorm room phone number. Before that moment, I did not have a need for a cell phone, but I knew I needed one now. I drove to Walgreens and purchased something called a TracFone. It was the fastest and easiest phone to get because Walgreens was only a few feet from the university. It took a few days, but she called me in my room, and I gave her my new number so she could contact me anytime. I finally asked her out, and she gladly accepted.

It was a beautiful Saturday night, and I knew I had to bring my A game. I had purchased new clothes and had new cologne. I felt this night would be special except for one thing: my car. I still drove the same car I had driven in high school, a 1992 Chevrolet Beretta. I didn't know how Keshia would feel about riding in an older car, although I kept it in tremendous shape. Earlier that day, I took it to the car wash and got every speck of dirt off that I could. I bought several air fresheners and put them throughout the car. I also put enough wax and Tire Wet on that car that someone would think it was brand-new. I met her downstairs in her dorm lobby, and she looked great. I walked her to my car and thought for sure she was going to walk away. Much to my surprise, she didn't. She told me she wasn't worried about what I drove and was looking forward to having a good time. At this moment, I knew she was special. I took her to Cracker Barrel for our first date.

Over the next few weeks, we began to develop a real connection. As the semester went by, we grew closer and closer. By the end of that semester, my grades had done a complete 360. I was as focused as I ever was in my studies and ended up making the dean's list. I had also become the overnight leader at my job. Everything was back on track, and I couldn't be happier.

After that second semester was over, I had a chance to visit Keshia's home in Gulfport, MS and speak with her parents. She lived near the beach, and I instantly fell in love with the Gulf Coast. This was my first time visiting, and I did not realize how much different the Gulf Coast was compared to the rest of the state. Everywhere that the eye could see, there were beautiful palm trees, radiant skies, white sand, and of course the gulf itself. Every chance I got that summer, I drove to the coast not only to enjoy the beautiful scenery but more importantly to spend time with Keshia. Life had given my lemons, but at that point I could honestly say I was making lemonade.

CHAPTER 7

The Game Changer

My freshman year of college was in the books, the summer had passed, and it was now time for the start of my sophomore year. One night when I was off, Keshia called me and told me she was sick. She asked me if I would take her to get some medicine. Of course I obliged, and we were on our way. I asked her where she would like to go, and she said Walmart. There was one about a mile from the university, so that was where we went. It was late at night, it was my only night off, and I was tired, but there was no way I was going to mess up my new relationship. She sent me in for some medicine, and I told her I would be right back.

I walked over to the pharmacy and heard a familiar sound. I had heard that sound when I was fifteen years old, stocking groceries at Save-A-Lot. I heard that sound every night at my current job. I heard the sweet sound of box cutters cutting open boxes and merchandise going on shelves. I took a moment and walked around the store. I saw more than groceries being stocked away. I saw toys, sporting goods, electronics, automotive, and apparel. It sounded like a symphony, and I wanted in. At that moment, I knew there was no question: I had to be a part of this.

I saw someone who had the look of a manager standing in the grocery department; his name was Haskel. I approached him and told him what I did, my past experiences, and that I was interested in becoming part of the overnight team. He took my information and told me he would pass it along.

I got back to the car, and needless to say Keshia was not too happy. She told me she had been sitting there for over an hour, waiting on me. She said she had called my phone, and I didn't answer. I must have put it on silent because when I looked at it, I saw fifteen missed calls. To make matters worse, I came out with no medicine. While Keshia was outside sick in my car, I was in Walmart trying to get a job. I told her I got sidetracked talking and apologized. I ran back in, got the medicine, and then drove her back to her dorm. She was mad when she got out and went back into her dorm. I felt bad about leaving her alone for an hour, so I hoped the hour that I had spent talking to Haskel was not in vain.

The next morning, I got a phone call from someone named Don. He said he was the assistant manager of grocery, and he wanted me to come in for an interview that day. After class, I went to an interview, and he hired me as an overnight stocker on the spot. He told me that after the background check and drug test came back, he wanted me to begin immediately. The store was only a year old, sales had taken off, and they were short-handed. I then had the inevitable task of informing Piggly Wiggly that I would be putting in my two weeks' notice because I had found another job. After class, I drove to the store and informed the store leadership of my decision. I could sense some disappointment, but they understood. I felt as though this was the right decision for my future, and I couldn't wait to start my new job.

A week later, I received a call from a lady named Sandy to come in for orientation on Tuesday. I told her I would be there with bells on! I penciled it in on my calendar: "Orientation at Walmart on Tuesday, September 11, 2001, at 9:00 a.m." I had moved most of my classes to the afternoon due to all the hardcore lessons I'd learned during my freshman year, so this would not be an issue. As I arrived to the store for orientation, I was falling deeper in love with my new company. When I entered the store, I immediately smelled the fresh aroma of someone grilling. In this particular store, there was a restaurant called the Radio Grill just past the grocery entrance. They served burgers, hotdogs, fries, and a vast array of other snacks. I looked inside and noticed that the people working there were wearing Walmart vests or aprons. Both were light blue, and they had the phrase "Every Day Low Prices Always" in red written on them. Their name badges were the colors of the American flag. I stepped in, introduced myself, and asked where the training room was. The employees told me, and I was on my way.

As I passed the Radio Grill, I smelled the aroma of freshly baked bread and produce. The fresh areas were beautiful. It looked like paradise compared to what I had seen at other grocery stores. I made my way through dry grocery, apparel, the backroom, and then the training room. Sandy introduced me to a gentleman named Franklin, the personnel manager. She then stated she was the training coordinator. He welcomed me to Walmart and then began orientation with me and two other new employees. One of the first things he explained to me was that they did not use the term *employee* but rather *associate*. He said at Walmart, we were one big family, and we worked for each other regardless of job titles. The first part of orientation ended at noon, so Sandy and Franklin sent us to lunch.

28

I wasn't that hungry due to excitement, so I decided I would look around the store for an hour. I had already seen the food side, so I walked through toys, sporting goods, automotive, and one of my personal favorites, lawn and garden. As I was heading back to the training room from lunch, I made one final stop in electronics. I looked at the live feed on the TV display area and saw smoke coming from a building in New York City. There were quite a few people around, so I knew something had to be wrong. I learned that planes had collided with several buildings, causing several casualties. The headline also mentioned that it was a terrorist attack and that officials were immediately grounding all aircrafts throughout the United States. It was a very disturbing moment for me and a very disturbing moment for our nation. To me, it was almost like the Earth stood still.

As I returned to the training room, it was hard to concentrate, but I knew I had to make it through, so orientation continued. Franklin sat me down at a computer and told me that I had thirty to forty CBL modules to complete. I didn't know the Walmart lingo yet, so I asked what a CBL was. He chuckled but then told me it was computer-based learning, designed to enhance my skills and make me successful at Walmart. The modules included safety procedures and an introduction into the policies at Walmart. He mentioned that it would take me a few days to finish them. I told him that I would have them finished by tomorrow. He was thrilled to hear this and appreciated the commitment to getting done quickly.

The next day, I did exactly what I said and finished by noon. Franklin then told me that I would be starting overnight the next night. He handed me a new vest, a box cutter, a back brace, and knee pads. He gave me a schedule and wished me good luck. As I left personnel, I saw this gentleman coming toward me in a white shirt, tie, slacks, and Walmart name badge. My first thought was trying to figure out how he could get any work done in a shirt and tie, but as he got closer, I realized he was the store manager. He was tall and clean-cut. He shook my hand and introduced himself. He told me he was happy to have me part of his team, and he wanted to see big things out of me. I told him, "Don't worry, you will." At that moment, I knew what I wanted to do. I wanted to come to work and dress in slacks, collar shirts, and ties. I wanted to manage a large retail store. I wanted people to look up to me. I wanted to make his money. I was determined to become him. So it began.

CHAPTER 8

A New Team

When the time came for me to begin overnight, I could feel the anticipation building all day. In business class, the professor talked about successful businesses, including Walmart. In his lecture, he discussed in detail Walmart's rise from the bottom to the top. He mentioned to the class that Walmart was number one on Forbes's list of America's most admired companies. The accolades that he mentioned were overwhelming, and I couldn't help but smile knowing that I was now part of the world's largest retailer. After class was finished for the day, I got dressed for work and drove to the store. My shift didn't start until 10:00 p.m., but I was so eager and did not want to be late, so I arrived at 9:00. I was nervous and excited at the same time. Then it was time.

I clocked in and sat in the lounge, where the overnight meeting was held nightly. At 10:00, assistant managers Don and Jack walked in and introduced themselves to me before beginning the meeting. After they finished covering the store's financials and other business, they gave us our assignments for the night. I was assigned to the juice, water, and soda aisles to stock. We ended the meeting with a cheer.

After that meeting, I spoke with the leader of the overnight grocery team, Haskel; several people called him Ham for some reason. It was good to see him because he was instrumental in me getting the job. He asked me if I needed to be partnered with someone because I was new. I told him I had experience, so I knew how to stock, but I needed to know how things were done on the overnight shift. He then introduced me to the overnight grocery team, which included Donnie, who was a master at stocking juice; Gina, who was the snack queen; Jennifer, who was the rice aisle connoisseur; Chris, who was our baking aisle specialist; Mike, who was our canned goods king; Paul, who was our coffee aisle specialist; and Joseph, who was a floater.

Ham explained that this was not everyone, just the associates who were working that night. He showed me their procedures, which were similar to what I had done in the past, including spotting merchandise on the floor. After spotting, we would stack all the pallets neatly, gather all plastic and trash, and take the back for processing. We then would take a dust broom and sweep through all the aisles. All this had to be done before midnight, which was our first fifteen-minute break. Everyone went to break except for me. There was so much merchandise down the aisles that made me question whether I could get it done. I started working my assigned aisles to get a head start. When everyone came from break, including Ham, they asked why I didn't take a break. I told them I was not built that way. I would take a break when I was done or legally required to do so. I flew through that freight as fast as I could, knowing I had to prove myself. When I finished, all that was left was zoning. This included straightening all merchandise and making it shoppable for customers.

As I pounded my chest inside my head thinking I was the man, I walked past the canned vegetable aisle to notice it was stocked and zoned. I walked past the coffee aisle, and it was stocked and zoned. Some of the others were still being worked on. I asked them how they had finished so fast. They told me they didn't play around and had other departments to work other than just one aisle. That was an eye-opening moment for me because I knew I was not the man—they were the men. I had to up my game. That store had beasts working in grocery, and I was just a gazelle. I told myself that this was not going to work, and I had better get faster. I had always been the hardest worker in the room, and that was not about to change now.

When I got off that morning, Keshia asked me how it went. I told her it was terrible and didn't want to talk about it, but I also assured her there were no worries. I got this. After I got off, I slept, went to class from 2:00 p.m. to 9:00 p.m., and then prepared to get back to work. That night was a lot different. I did exactly what I said and made sure no one outworked me, essentially making me the fastest person on the team in my second night. Ham was so impressed that got Don to watch me stock. Both were apparently in awe because they started yelling down the grocery aisles for everyone to take notes. Most stockers didn't like that, so I was labeled a brown-noser and a suck-up. I didn't care. I was there to work, I was there to be the best, and after meeting the current store manager, I was there to become a store manager.

As time went on, I continued to work hard, which meant I got faster, I got smarter, and eventually I got my first promotion. Three months passed, and I was now a support manager, which meant I was in charge of the night crew, working alongside the salaried assistant manager. It was great making more money, but it was even better to receive the promotion. I knew this was not my last promotion but rather a stepping stone onto the next one. At the time, assistant managers rotated every six months, so it was time for a new set of managers overnight. Don and Jack transitioned to days. We were then introduced to assistant managers Clyde and Murphy. Clyde was tall, slender, and very energetic. He had a wealth of knowledge and had a smoldering intensity when necessary. Murphy was tall, husky, and very intimidating. Everyone, including some of our customers, knew to not cross Murphy! I had the opportunity to learn from both of them over the next six months. Clyde taught me how to create a winning team by boosting and maintaining associate morale. He also taught me how to be a maverick with merchandise. He taught me how to get creative when building displays and how to increase sales. He taught me the fundamentals of being an assistant manager in a high-volume store. Clyde and I also had a similar taste in food, so I was assigned lunch duty nightly. Most of the time we settled on either Wendy's or Krystal's. Murphy taught me his smoldering intensity. He taught me when to turn it on and when to turn off. If things were not going well, he taught me how to prioritize and make good decisions by putting associates in the departments where they were fast. He also taught me how to get the work finished in the face of adversity such as call-ins.

Every day and night posed a new challenge. Classes were getting harder, and so was work. I had a lot of responsibilities, which meant that relationships began to suffer. I was not talking to my mother and family as much because I was in class, sleeping, or at work. I had even changed my voicemail on my phone to say that exact statement. One relationship that did not suffer was the one with the angel I had met in Nutrition class. She was so supportive of everything I did and admired the fact that I worked hard. She told me I reminded her of her father because he always worked hard for his family to have a better life. I spent every free second I got with her. If I had a night off, we studied together in the library or went on a date. If we weren't on a date, we would sneak off in the middle of the night, head to Krystal's, sit in my car, and talk for hours.

As that semester came to a close, I had achieved much success, but I knew I was not finished yet. I knew that I was going to do whatever it took to finish my degree, and I knew I was going to do whatever it took to become a store manager. I had a long road ahead and knew I had to find ways to work harder and smarter. I had to find new ways to balance school, my job, and relationships. I finished my prerequisites for my accounting degree and was about to begin my core coursework, so the fun for me was only beginning.

CHAPTER 9

Summertime

I had decided to take courses over the summer to lighten my load during the fall semester. There were pros and cons that I weighed before ultimately deciding to go. I knew that I would not have to take as many hours in the fall, which would enable me to have more time for relationships and more time that I could work. The biggest downfall was the cost of school during the summer. At that time, scholarships and federal grants were not allowed to be used during summer semesters because they were deemed optional. The only options were to pay upfront or take out a loan, which was what I did. I knew when I graduated, I was going to land this big job being a store manager, so the loan didn't matter.

I had the time of my life that summer. I took several courses and made good grades. My girlfriend had moved back home for the summer, so I visited her every chance I got. Most of the time I let her know I was coming, but there were a few times when I did not. She had a summer job working at an arcade in the mall. Often I would appear and surprise her at her job. She was always happy to see me when I came down. I enjoyed walks on the beach, time spent with her family, and above all else enjoyed time with her. One of our favorite things to do was drive to New Orleans and visit Audubon Zoo. Both of us really enjoyed seeing the animals but enjoyed spending time with each other more. We even decided to go to the world famous Bourbon Street a few times. We met some very interesting people each time we went, and we always had a good time. We documented our adventures by posing and taking photos with our single-use camera. Sometimes it was hard to get good pictures because we had to wind the camera up each time and stand pretty close to our target in order to get a good shot. We were talking selfies before they were called selfies. We also enjoyed going to visit the Grand Casino in Gulfport to eat. Every time we entered, we had to get a wristband just to walk to the restaurant because we had to walk past all the slot machines, and we were not old enough to gamble. Casino leadership made sure we had restraints. They had the best buffet on the Gulf Coast in my opinion. I was introduced to prime rib, crab legs, and several other delicacies that I had never had. I also got the chance to go to a live WWE wrestling event for the first time. I have always been a big wrestling fan since I was a child. I got a chance to see several of the major stars, including the WWE Undisputed Heavyweight Champion at the time, Triple H.

However, it seemed I always had to cut our time short because I had to be back at work at 10:00 p.m. that night. It was an hour drive from the coast back to the university, but I didn't care. I enjoyed spending time with my angel. Each drive back got longer and longer. Working overnight does something to your body, no matter how young you are. It makes you tired and restless. There were plenty of instances where I almost ran off the road due to falling asleep, but it was almost like an angel was watching over me each time. As summer raged on and I fell more and more for Keshia, I felt like I was on top of the world. I was tired, but it felt great! I was visiting her two or three times a week, creating a new adventure every time. It was also an adventure at work every night that summer.

During that summer, with the assistance of the overnight assistant managers, we developed the fiercest overnight team that the store had ever seen. We were firing on all cylinders and could not be stopped, achieving feats that had never been done in that store. We were getting freight worked in record times. We reduced the amount of inventory we carried in the backroom, and we were taking care of our customers better than ever. Every Wednesday night, Clyde would go to personnel and pass out our paychecks at midnight. One night as I went in to get mine, he told me that the store manager wanted to see me in the morning. Class didn't begin until noon the next day, so it wasn't a problem. I thought to myself, *This can't be good. Why does he want to see an overnight associate when he has an entire store to run? Am I about to get fired? What did I do?* As the night ended, I waited for him in his office.

He came in, sat down, and then stared at me without saying a word. After about three minutes of silence, he extended his hand and said, "I see you." He said he was in awe of what we were doing overnight. We had single-handedly turned his store around and made his job much easier. He also told me that it was due to my leadership. I told him that it was the assistant managers. He then told me that he thought the same thing, but those same managers told him that it was me. I thanked him and then told him that I had aspirations to be a store manager like him. His office phone rang, but he did not pick it up. He continued and told me not to be like him, but rather create my own path because everyone's journey was different. As he talked, the phone continued to ring, so I looked down and asked him if he wanted me to get it. He shook my hand again and then sent me away, stating he had to take the call because it was his district manager. Although our conversation was short, it had a major impact on the way I approached my job. I felt appreciated, and I felt like I needed to do more.

CHAPTER 10
Mission Accomplished

When my junior year began in college, I had decided to venture out on my own and move off campus. I rented a very small apartment that was walking distance to the campus. The apartment would allow me privacy and, more importantly, allow me to get uninterrupted sleep after working overnight. A friend from work, Robert always referred to my apartment as Small-Mart because of its incredibly small kitchen and living room. I told him it wouldn't always be like this and that it was temporary. He always gave me a few laughs whenever we met. I could not have asked for a better coworker or a better friend.

Although it felt good to have my own place, I must admit adversity began to sink in. I had a set of courses so tough that even the university president would question the validity of my schedule. What made it tougher was that most of these courses were only offered during certain times, so I had no choice but to take them at those times. This normally would not be a problem, but of course I was working overnight at the time. Work got tougher. There was a lot of turnover, which meant a lot of new faces who required training.

This meant less productivity, which meant a ton of added stress for me. I also had to make time for my relationship. I lost a ton of weight. When I visited my mother, she would always ask if I was okay. She would then send me back to college with a car full of groceries and told me to eat something. She always sent my favorites.

Every day was a new challenge. If I wasn't in class, I was working. By my junior year, I was working roughly forty-eight hours a week. I had fallen in love with the company I was working for and knew where I wanted to take my career. If I wasn't working or in class, I was studying. In between all that, I spent all the time that I could with Keshia. Whether we were studying together or going to the movies, I cherished every moment. The one person who I did not make time for was me. All my college classmates were having the time of their lives. They were going out and partying almost every night, whereas I was busy working. I was jealous I must admit, but I knew I had to do what I had to do to get to where I wanted to be. The party could wait, but this degree and jump starting my career could not.

As my senior year in college approached, it was decision time. I was told by so many people that Walmart was not the place to be, or for that matter to start a career. I was told that I would be selling myself short and should pursue another line of work. I usually drowned out all the noise and made my own decisions, but this time I did not. After listening to so much advice from different individuals, I decided I would be a school teacher. I would finish my degree, get the necessary certifications, and then get a job teaching. By this time, we had again switched managers overnight at work. Assistant managers Tommy and Johnny were assigned to overnights during my senior year. Johnny, or John for short, was a former store manager and had a wealth of knowledge. He was very mature and always helped guide me to the right decisions inside the workplace. One night we were discussing future plans, and he offered me some advice that sounded very familiar. He told me that he would support me no matter what, but he strongly believed I should stay with my current company and apply for the management program. He told me that he saw something in me that he saw in himself: drive and ambition. He then told me something that would resonate with me for years to come. He told me to do what I had to do to get to where I wanted to be. Deep inside, I wanted to be a store manager—period. There was no debate, no internal discussion, and definitely no other option than becoming a Walmart store manager. Although I knew what I wanted to do, I told him that I would think it over, and in a few weeks I would make my final decision.

A few weeks passed, and it was decision time, but I had something very important to do before then. I was set to become the first person in my family to graduate from a university. I had worked hard and had earned a bachelor of science in business administration. I was set to graduate on a cold December morning in 2003. When I woke up that morning, I was so nervous I could not even eat. My mother and my extended family were set to attend my graduation, and I wanted to show all of them that with hard work and ambition, nothing was unachievable. My mother wanted to see me before I walked across the stage, so she and a close cousin, Jennifer, arrived at my apartment early. She told me she was proud of me and couldn't wait to hear my name called. I shed a tear and told her that if it was not for her, I wouldn't be the man that I had become. When we arrived on campus, we decided to take a picture in front of the main fountain at the university. As Mom and I posed, a gust of wind blew, by causing my hat to fall into the fountain. I quickly tried to grab it, but it was already soaked. Jennifer said, "No worries. I got you." She purchased a hair dryer, found an outlet, dried my hat, and had me up and running at no time.

Nonetheless, Mom gave me a hug, wished me luck, and told me she loved me and couldn't be prouder. They sat in the stands, and I went to prepare with the rest of my class of 2003. As I stood in that tunnel and the graduation music began to play, I thought, *This is only the beginning of the journey.* Playtime was over, and now it was time to truly get to work. However, I was going to enjoy this moment that I had earned. As I sat in my seat, I glanced around the coliseum to find my family. They weren't too hard to find because of all the noise they were making by calling my name. I was so excited to see all of them. My mother, my aunts, and several cousins had come out to see me graduate from college. After about two hours' worth of speeches and other graduation festivities, it was time. When the master of ceremony called my name, I cried tears of joy. As my family celebrated with pride and joy, I shook the university president's hand as he handed me my degree. I had weathered the storm. I had stayed the course and completed the journey. I was now an official graduate of the University of Southern Mississippi. After three long years, I earned a BSBA. I could now officially say, mission accomplished!

CHAPTER 11

Assistant Manager Trainee

After I graduated, I informed most of the store's management team that I wanted to become an assistant manager. Most of them said the same thing, which was that it was about time. I applied to get into the Walmart management program in late December. Weeks passed, and I still didn't hear anything. In January 2004, I was on the scissor lift in the garden center, putting grills on the top shelf when my cell phone started ringing. It was midnight, so naturally I wondered who was calling. I didn't recognize the number but answered anyway because it could be an emergency. It was the district manager. He asked me how I was doing and then told me that he was putting me into the management program in February. He told me that the store manager believed I had what it took, and so did he. I told him I was excited, couldn't be happier, and was eager to get started. After I hung up the phone, I began shouting for joy, jumping up and down on the scissor lift, but I quickly stopped. I realized two things: first, I shouldn't have answered my phone on a scissor lift that high in the air, and second, I definitely should not be jumping up and down on a scissor lift that high in the air!

EXT. 170

As soon as I got down out of the lift, I ran to tell Assistant Manager Clyde. I then called Keshia to let her know. It was a Monday morning, and I knew she would be asleep, but I couldn't contain my excitement. She had graduated a semester before me and was teaching in Jackson, Mississippi, so I couldn't exactly tell her face-to-face. She told me she was proud of me, but she had to work tomorrow. I told her I understood and went and finished my shift. Apparently, word got around fast because as I was clocking out, everyone congratulated me and gave me a pat on the back. Robert even gave me a hug and told me to not let assistant manager be it. He told me to stay the course and finish the journey. He then said that now I could afford to move out of Small-Mart. After a brief laugh, I left, got in my car, and drove home.

I felt like a little kid in a candy store. I felt as though I could do anything. I felt as though I had arrived again. When I got back to my apartment, I called my mother and told her. She told me that I continue to make her proud, and she could not have asked for a better son. I told her that this was only the beginning. I worked as hard as I could over the next few weeks to leave my stamp on the store, but most importantly on the overnight team I was about to leave behind. Most of them were incredibly talented and had bright futures ahead of them. My final night was filled with high-fives and a lunch send-off for the ages. Almost everyone was happy for me, except a few who kept telling me that I was making a mistake and that Walmart was not the place to be. I told them thanks for the advice, but I was going to keep growing, and I was going to ride this train until the wheels fell off. The overnight assistant manager, John, let me leave shortly after lunch. As he walked me out the door, he shook my hand and told me to not look back and keep moving forward. I didn't speak any words but simply gave him a thumbs-up and walked away. As I drove to my apartment, I prayed that I would be successful on this new journey,

45

knowing that this was only the beginning and that there was much more to come.

Monday morning arrived, and it was finally time to get to work. Luckily for me, I was selected to train at the store across town, which meant I did not have to move. When I arrived at the store, I was met at the front door by Benjamin. He shook my hand, welcomed me, and escorted me to the training room in the grocery receiving area. There were a total of eight other trainees who were in my class from various stores across southern Mississippi: Gary, Kim, Tonya, Christi, Brian, Tom, and Alex. After we introduced ourselves, we told stories of our backgrounds. It was so amazing to hear that I was in a room of former stockers, customer service managers, department managers, and even a loss prevention manager. It was also amazing to hear that all of them had similar career aspirations. Most of them wanted to be store managers or greater. Most of them also told stories about what they would buy when they became store managers, which mainly included expensive cars and houses. All that was nice, but I was always taught to crawl before I could walk. We all had dreams, but I had to hit the first goal, which was making it through assistant manager training.

Benjamin introduced himself as an assistant manager rising star and the assistant manager trainee facilitator. He told us his background, including how long he had been with the company. It was amazing to hear he had been with the company over fifteen years; I was going on my third year. He handed us a journal and told us to never lose it. We would need it to record daily financial data and our completed tasks. He also outlined our agenda for the next sixteen weeks. Some important advice he gave us was to never stop learning, and to learn on our own. He told us to lean on each other and lean on the associates in the store, including department managers and other assistant managers. He then wished us luck and told us to get started on our computer-based learning, which would take almost a week to finish. For an entire week, I worked diligently to finish my modules timely so I would be prepared for what would come next. It was 3:00 p.m. on Friday, and I had finally finished. Benjamin told me I could enjoy my weekend early because there wouldn't be many weekends off when I officially became an assistant manager. I told him I was grateful, but I was going to spend the last two hours on the sales floor learning. I met some incredible associates, including loss prevention associates, sales associates, and department managers.

There were two associates I met who had an immediate impact on me. The first was a department manager, Tammy. She worked over in apparel and had a wealth of knowledge. She told me to come work with her during my spare time, and she would show me what it was like on the sales floor in a high-volume store. I gladly accepted this invitation because I knew nothing about apparel. The second associate who would have an immediate impact was a department manager, Johnny. He was responsible for pets, paper, and chemicals. He echoed what Tammy said and invited me to come work with him. I gladly accepted his invitation. After I took one last tour around the store, I knew that the rest of my training was going to be incredible because I had associates on my side, and they were willing to put in the time and help train me. I drove back to my apartment and relaxed for the weekend.

I woke up early Saturday morning, got dressed, and drove two hours to Jackson to spend time with my angel, Keshia. I did not get a chance to see her much because she was working there, and I was working two and a half hours away. One of our favorite things to do was see movies. Our favorite theater was Tinseltown. We would enjoy candy, popcorn, soda, and whatever else made her happy. One of the mack daddy moves that I always pulled was to make sure that I purchased only one soda so we could use two straws. This made her smile. We also enjoyed going out to eat at several restaurants, but our favorite was O'Charley's. It was close to Tinseltown, so we didn't have to drive far. Every weekend was a challenge because in the back of my mind, I knew I had to get back to work hours away, and I did not like leaving her alone. Although she was living in a very nice gated community, I still did not like her there by herself. We were far away from each other, but our relationship kept getting better. She always told me to be careful and to let her know when I made it home because she did not want to lose me.

When Monday mornings approached, I knew I had to refocus and get myself back to work. The store was in the middle of a remodel during management training, so I was able to learn a lot about setting modulars, moving fixtures, and several other intangibles that were not taught on computer-based learning. We were allowed to attend the store's management meeting from time to time. The meeting was held in a food retail space near the back of the store. I would hear from the store's senior leadership, including the store manager, about the day's agenda. We also heard about the store's financials so we could record the data in our journals.

Every day, after I finished my assigned tasks as outlined on my training agenda, I would go and find Tammy in apparel. She would teach me all the basics I did not know, including how to do price changes, how to flag counters properly, and how to conduct inventory in her area. She never said anything, but every now and then, I could tell she would get a little frustrated with me because I asked a ton of questions. I could sense this and decided to scale back a little and help her with her daily tasks. As I learned, I helped her stock, zone, and manage her area.

I often engaged John and asked questions that would help me be successful. He took time and made me understand what shrink was in a retail store. Some of the other trainees would often ask where I would disappear to every day, and I told them that I was learning on the sales floor. One of the trainees would take the opportunity to leave the store once the training agenda was complete, but not me. I wanted to learn—I had to learn to be successful. As I have stated many times before, I was not always the smartest person in the room, but I was always the person who worked the hardest.

After fifteen weeks, we were slated to learn our fate. We were all anxious because we knew we were about to be told what store we would go to after completing our management training. At the time, management trainees could be placed anywhere in the district. Monday went by, and we were told nothing. Tuesday went by, and still nothing. Wednesday and Thursday went by, and we didn't know where we were headed. Finally on Friday, we were told that there would be one-on-one meetings in the district manager's office later that day, and we would be told where we are going.

After lunch, Benjamin and the district manager called me to the office. I stood as they sat and awaited their decision. Benjamin told me that he noticed the intangibles. He noticed the extra work and extra learning I put in. The district manager told me he had heard nothing but good things about me. Both of them then informed me that I was going to remain in that store as an assistant manager! This was the best news that I could have received. I would not have to move, and I was already familiar with the store. I almost shed a tear but very quickly got back my composure. I shook their hands and told them I would not let them down. I was the last trainee to learn his or her fate, so they were all waiting for me in the hallway when I came out of the office. They shared where they were going. All of them were going to other stores in the district except for me. They asked how I pulled it off. I told them I didn't pull it off—I simply worked hard.

Tammy and Johnny both found me and told me how proud they were of me, adding they could not wait to work with me. As the weekend commenced, I could not wait to let Keshia know the wonderful news. When I arrived back in Jackson and told her, she jumped for joy. She also had some news to share with me. She had gotten a teaching job on the Mississippi Gulf Coast. It was like all the stars were aligning at once. The Gulf Coast was only an hour away from where I was working, and it had become my favorite part of the state. We both were excited and eager for what was to come. I graduated from management training along with the rest of my class. We all vowed to keep in contact with each other no matter what. We also vowed to each be successful and become the best that we could be.

As I was leaving for the day, I was called into the store manager's office. There sat the store manager and his comanagers, Pat and Jim. They congratulated me and told me they were looking for big things from me. They told me that they were putting me in apparel for my first area. I thought this was interesting because I would now be managing one of the individuals who mentored me during the training, but I was up for the challenge. Jim told me he was the general merchandise co-manager and that I would report to him. He handed me a Motorola two-way radio, the thickest set of keys in history, and a new name badge with the words "assistant manager" written on it. He then told me to enjoy the weekend, and he would see me Monday morning.

As I left, I made an internal pact with myself that I was going to make it, and I was going to become store manager. I was going to do it in three steps. First, I would become an assistant manager and be successful at it. Second, I would become a co-manager and be successful at it. I would then become store manager and be successful at it. Failing was not an option, and I was up for the challenge. I was born for this.

CHAPTER 12

Assistant Manager

Monday morning arrived, and it was time. I woke up, got dressed, and arrived an hour early for my shift. There was no official routine or blueprint at the time that outlined my daily tasks, so I had to develop my own. When 7:00 a.m. arrived, I went around, introduced myself to the associates I did not know, and then went to work. As a rookie assistant manager, I worked in the department where I was most comfortable, which was with Tammy. I started doing exactly what I was doing before, which was putting up merchandise and replacing signing. When 8:00 a.m. arrived, I was called to the management meeting. As I took my seat, the store manager introduced me to everyone and said he was excited to have me on the team. He then covered the previous day's store manager recap. He mentioned sales, wage percentage, and inventory levels, among other things. With the exception of sales, most of the language that he used seemed foreign to me. I immediately identified this as an area of opportunity that I needed to improve upon. Both co-managers then assigned us notes and gave us our agendas for the day. By the time they were finished, I had a notepad full of tasks that needed to be completed that day. Once we adjourned from the meeting, I started on my notes.

I wanted to shine, and I wanted to get them completed early. About an hour later, Jim approached me and asked me what I was doing. I told him I was completing my notes. He then asked who was helping me, and I told him no one. He pulled me to the side and reminded me that my name badge now said assistant manager. He told me that I would never be successful as a manager trying to get everything done on my own. Although I may have taken offense to what he said, deep inside I knew he was right. I started to think back to my first job, when I was doing all the work and everyone else was standing around. It was my first day as assistant manager, and my supervisor had already gotten on to me about not delegating. I had to change the narrative quickly. I called a meeting with all the department managers in apparel, which included Carol, Lisa, Ann, and Tammy. I gave them all their notes and gave them a time to be completed. Most of them mentioned that they had other daily tasks they had to attend to, including setting modulars and doing price changes. I told them I understood, but these notes had to be done no matter what. I then completed the notes that were unique to assistant managers and could not be delegated.

After lunch, I went to follow up on the notes I had assigned out. I was surprised when I learned that not one single note that I had assigned was done. I asked the department managers individually why, and they all said the same thing they had told me before. Needless to say, I wasn't very happy. Jim then called me to the side and told me that I had to do a better job of managing people in order to get things done. I apologized and told him that I understood and that it wouldn't happen again. I went home that night thinking I was a failure. I was very restless and couldn't sleep. I was also very anxious to get back to work so I could correct what had happened the previous day.

The next day, I arrived at work early and completed all the notes from the previous day myself. We had our management meeting. I received a fresh set of notes, and we adjourned. I then called another meeting with my apparel team. My tone was slightly different than it was the day before. This time, I lined out expectations with intensity. I told them everything stopped until these notes were completed. I was told the same thing I was told before, which was they had too much to do. I didn't utter a word but simply gave them a blank stare and walked away. I came back ten minutes later to follow up and see whether the notes were started, and to my surprise they were all getting after them. They were doing what I had asked, and they were doing it fast. In an hour, all the notes were completed, and I couldn't have been happier. I asked all of them how they were able to get done so fast. They told me teamwork made the dream work. I thanked them for their hard work and mentioned to them that I would like to see the same intensity every day, no matter what. As time went on, the associates and I developed a great relationship, albeit with a few setbacks. I experienced turnover at a higher rate than I expected, I had to have a few performance-related discussions with some of the associates, and I had my own personal new-to-role growing pains as well.

During my time as apparel assistant manager, one of the other managers at the bakery and deli took an emergency leave of absence, so I was assigned that area as well. During my time in fresh, I learned the basics but also learned a lot about compliance. Fresh was different than any other part of the store, so I had to lean on my associates quite a bit to be successful. Eventually, apparel was given to another assistant manager, and I remained at fresh for the rest of my rotation.

At the time, assistant managers stayed in their area for six months and then rotated to another area. Once my first six months were over, I was moved to the consumables area. There, I had responsibility for health and beauty, cosmetics, pharmacy, paper, chemicals, and pets. I was very excited to have this area because I was comfortable here. Another perk of having this area was that John was one of the department managers in this area. John was instrumental in helping me grow from trainee to manager. Although I was excited, I knew going in I had work to do. Inventory levels were extremely high in the backroom, and the area was short handed due to turnover. Turnover was high at the store mainly because it was a college town. Once most of the associates who were students graduated, a lot of them moved on to other careers. Nonetheless, I was up for the challenge. In order to be successful, I had to have associates to get the work done, so one of the first things I did when I took over consumables was staff the area. I recruited from within but also brought aboard some new talent as well. I had a certain amount of wages and hours to spend, so I had to be strategic with anyone I hired. By partnering with the personnel manager, I was able to get staffed within a matter of weeks, and the results were almost immediate. Morale among the department managers went up, and inventory levels in the backroom went down. The area was not perfect by any means, but it was much better in stock. The store manager and the co-managers were satisfied with my performance and made it a point to tell me so. Jim told me that he was going to make me one of his mentees. He told me he felt as though I had what it took to take my career to another level if I continued performing like I was. I humbly told him how much I appreciated it. He also told me that I would be remaining in this area for a while. I had a good thing going, and though he did not want to stall my growth, the store needed me here. I did not object and did as I was told.

Everything was working out great at work, but often when I left work, I felt alone and empty. I didn't have much time to hang out with friends, and I had hardly any time with Keshia. She was busy teaching on the Gulf Coast throughout the week, and I was busy working most weekends. It had been almost four years since we had met, and I wanted something more than just a relationship. I believed she did as well. In early 2005, I did what I never thought I would be able to do: I asked Keshia to marry me. She gladly accepted. I was overjoyed and a little nervous at the same time. Once I was alone, I began to second-guess myself. I pondered whether I had made the right decision. I had never been married before or lived with a woman outside of my mother. I wondered how we would be able to coexist with combined finances. I also realized I had missed a step in the "asking her to marry me" process. I did not consult her father, which was tradition. I knew by then I could not do anything about it because she had already broken the news to her family. Needless to say, I had a restless night.

I was off the next day, so I drove to my hometown and told my mother I was getting married. She was happy and sad at the same time. She told me no matter what, I would always be her baby. I could see the tears in her eyes as she said it. It almost felt like she was saying goodbye to me, so I assured her that was not the case. I told her this was simply a new chapter, and I would be fine.

Eventually I developed enough courage to apologize to her father for not asking his daughter's hand in marriage on the front side. Luckily, he accepted my apology and did not punch me in the gut like I anticipated. Over the next month, Keshia and I knew we had decisions to make. We had to set a date, discuss a budget for the wedding, decide where the ceremony would take place, and decide where we would live, among other things. We ultimately decided that we would get married that summer, which gave us six months to prepare.

Back at work, things continued to go well, and I grew as a manager. There were days that I experienced setbacks, and Jim had to pull me to the side and tell me what I needed to improve upon. I took each one of those conversations as an opportunity to learn and to grow. I also took those conversations as a wake-up call so I would not get fired. Every day was a new challenge. There were days when there was lack of staff due to multiple call-outs. There were days when I got in so much merchandise that I could not see the forest for the trees. There were days when I wanted to give up and days I wanted to give in, but I didn't. Every time I failed, I learned something new. I was learning how to be more disciplined and how to be a better manager. I had learned how to lead large teams and how to lean on them for guidance. I also experienced several firsts while I was at consumables. I experienced my first Black Friday event as assistant manager. I experienced my first annual inventory as assistant manager. I also experienced my first official regional visit as assistant manager. All these experiences molded me into being a better manager.

As the months went by, Keshia and I continued planning for our wedding. We were young, so we were heavily dependent on others for guidance. One of the biggest decisions that we made was to choose a venue for the wedding. We ultimately chose to have our wedding in front of God, family, and friends inside of a church. We wanted to be firmly rooted in God's house so that our marriage would last. We also knew that it would make our parents happy to see us get married in a traditional setting. We purchased a brand-new home and decided we would settle into our new life together in her hometown. After all, I had fallen in love with the Gulf Coast, and she could not have been happier.

On the eve of our wedding, the wedding party gathered at the church for practice. There, we got a chance to meet everyone whom we may not have known. After we practiced, we went to dinner and had a tremendous time. Most people hold bachelor and bachelorette parties the night before, but I had asked my best men, Slue and Rod, not to have one, and they did as requested. I wanted to relax and enjoy the evening alone. It was a restless night for me filled with questions and anxiety. When I woke up the next morning, all that doubt was erased. I had prayed and knew beyond a shadow of a doubt I had made the right decision. It was July 2, 2005, and I was about to get married!

I arrived at the church a little later than everyone else because I spent some time speaking to my mother and thanking her for getting me this far. It was she who had motivated me to make good grades through high school, earning several academic scholarships. It was she who had motivated me to keep fighting and earn my degree. It was also she who had motivated me to work harder than everyone and achieve things beyond my wildest dreams. As I was putting the final touches on my tuxedo, Robert from work walked up to me and put his hands on my shoulder. He told me he was proud of me. He had watched me grow from this skinny young kid who was a stocker to now an assistant manager who was about to get married. He also told me he was happy I could move out of Small-Mart and into something bigger.

Pastor Pilot, my two best men, and I entered the sanctuary that was full of coworkers, friends, and families. One of my best men, Rod, whom I have known since age five, kept whispering a few jokes in my ear to make me a little less nervous. This included reminding me about our old high school days and all the different adventures we had taken. I stood there and watched the wedding party enter, including the groomsmen, bridesmaids, and our parents. I then watched the mini groom and mini bride, who both were my cousins, enter. Both of them were children and extremely nervous. One carried both wedding rings on a soft, white designer pillow, and the other threw rose petals down in anticipation of the bride. Once they got to the front, one of them turned around and yelled out that the bride was coming. Everyone stood as "Here Comes the Bride" played throughout the church. As she entered, my tears immediately flowed. I couldn't believe it was actually happening, and I was getting married.

She got to the front with her father as the music stopped. Pastor Pilot asked who was giving her away. It seemed like the longest pause in history before her father acknowledged he was the one giving her away. I understood because that was his baby girl. I would have paused as well. As a matter of fact, I am not even sure I could give away my own daughter! Nonetheless, I extended my arm, and as she took it, she gave me a small wink to reassure me she loved me and wanted to be my bride. We could barely get through our vows due to all the tears we were shedding. After we placed rings on each other's fingers, Pastor Pilot told me to kiss my bride. This was the one part of the wedding I was dreading. I didn't want to kiss my bride in front of my mother, and I definitely did not want to kiss her in front of her father, who was staring a hole through me. I mustered up all the courage left in my body, lifted her veil, and went for it. After it was over, the first person I looked at was her father. In my eyes, all I could see was him cracking his knuckles and getting ready to take me behind the shed and relentlessly punch me in the gut. Eventually his frown turned into a smile, and ultimately he was happy for us.

Our wedding reception was very well received and was a thing of beauty. There was one minor hiccup that turned into the most eventful part of the wedding. It was time for the bride to toss her bouquet to potential new brides. In the honor of tradition, Keshia turned around and threw the bouquet. One of my cousins, who will remain nameless, went to catch the bouquet. As she jumped to catch it, the top of her dress came down briefly, exposing one of her breasts. Yes, everyone in the reception noticed. Luckily, back then there were no GIFs or memes, and social media did not exist outside of MySpace. If there had been, she would have been made famous almost instantly. To my knowledge, there is no footage of the incident, but unfortunately there were photos that eventually circulated to her friends and family.

I reflected on my life. I had graduated from college, I had become assistant manager, and now I had my bride. Things were looking up.

After we returned from our honeymoon, it was time for me to get back to work. It was good to have a week off to spend time with my bride. Returning to work was going to be a little different this time. Because we had decided to live in her hometown, I now had an hour commute. I wanted to transfer down to the Gulf Coast, but there were no openings yet. The first day back at work was not bad, but the drive was. I had to wake up much earlier to get dressed, and I got home a lot later than anticipated. As always, I adapted and was up for the challenge. The drive was long, but eventually I learned to deal with it.

On August 20, 2005, the Weather Channel informed the world of a disturbance that was forming and was on a direct path toward the Gulf Coast. I didn't think much of it because we had dealt with heavy inclement weather before. In the south, we had dealt with tornadoes, hurricanes, and even snow. In the coming days, the disturbance turned into Tropical Storm Katrina. It then strengthened and turned into Hurricane Katrina.

We were warned that this storm was going to be massive and life-threatening. We were told to evacuate the Gulf Coast on August 27. I drove home, and we packed essentials, boarded our brand-new home, and left. We decided to go my mother's home, which was also an hour away from work. We didn't have much of a choice due to all the hotels being booked already. I went to work on August 28. The city had decided that all businesses should close due to the incoming storm. Once we closed, I drove back to my mother's house to seek safety from the storm. When the morning of August 29 arrived, all I could see and feel was darkness even two hours away from the Gulf Coast in my hometown. There was no electricity and no means of communication. Katrina was there, and she was hammering South Mississippi.

Once Katrina moved on and it was safe enough, we looked outside, and all we could see was destruction. We saw trees down, power lines down, roofs off of houses, and houses completely destroyed. Keep in mind this was two hours away from the Gulf Coast. I had no way to contact my job and let them know I would not be able to make it to work because I was stuck in my hometown. I had no way of knowing whether our home was okay or whether Keshia's parents were okay because the phone lines were down. Her parents had sought asylum in her mother's hometown.

For two days, we were without electricity and without communication. We used that time to help clean up my mother's yard, which started with cutting a very large oak tree out of the road so we could drive. Once we were able to safely navigate the roads in my hometown, we cautiously drove where we could. As we had expected, there was more devastation. The main thing that was on my mind was getting back to work and getting back to our house. If Katrina had caused this much damage two hours away from the Gulf Coast, then we were afraid we had lost our home because we were only a few minutes from the Gulf of Mexico. We knew we were taking a chance with our attempt to drive back home, but it was a risk we were willing to take. Off we went. As we drove, we were finally able to get phone service and contact Keshia's parents. They were also driving back to the Gulf Coast. When we arrived, it was destruction the likes of which we had never seen. Houses were completely destroyed, power lines were still down, cars were piled on top of other cars, and boats that were meant to be in water now sat in the middle of highways. We knew what we were about to see when we arrived at home.

We decided to stop at Keshia's parents' house first. My brother-in-law informed us that it was bad; he had already been by our house to see what had happened. We reluctantly drove over to see our brand-new house almost destroyed. We had left behind two vehicles, and both of them had flooded. We had been in our home for only two months, and now we were going to have to start over. Although we were sad and upset, we were grateful to be alive. We had plenty of insurance on our home, so we knew we would be able to fix and rebuild it. It would simply take a while. We had no choice but to move in with her parents until we could find another alternative.

The next day, I called the store manager to let him know I was okay. He was happy, but he also said he needed me back immediately because they were going to reopen the store tomorrow. Most members of the management staff were still unable to get back to work because they were dealing with their own post-Katrina hardships. I told him I would be there. He then told me there was one other small detail. He informed me that I would be going overnight for the foreseeable future. The other overnight managers had sought asylum out of state, so he did not have anyone to manage overnights. We were at a twenty-four-hour store, so there had to be leadership. I told him I was up for the challenge and would be there tomorrow night.

I spent the next day salvaging what I could from our home, but then it was time. I had an hour drive to my job, so off I went. When I arrived, just as I had anticipated, we were short staffed. More than half of the workforce hadn't returned to work, and we had less than half of the management staff to work with for both days and nights. Although I had a ton of experience working overnight, that experience did not matter without enough associates to get the work done. We concentrated on what the customers needed. We made sure we stocked groceries, consumables, and some portions of the general merchandise side. We left apparel, domestics, and other nonessential departments such as toys. Customers needed water, not electronics. They needed formula for their babies, not garden center items. We made sure the store was stocked and zoned to the best of our abilities. As 7:00 a.m. approached, I met Patrick and James in the parking lot to let them know how the night went. They both said I had made the right decision concentrating on nonperishable items. They mentioned they had received word from several overnight associates that they would be returning soon. That was music to my ears. If there was one thing I knew I could do well, it was run overnights.

When I got off that morning, it dawned on me that I had worked all night and that I had to drive an hour with no sleep. About twenty minutes into the drive, my eyes began to get extremely heavy. Before I knew it, I was swerving all over the place, and I almost had an accident multiple times. Somehow by the grace of God, I made it home. I knew at that moment I could not drive like that every day. I would injure someone or injure myself. I did not know what I was going to do, but I knew I had to do something. A week later, I got a phone call from my friend Robert, whom I had worked with at a previous store. He told me he was calling to check on me and to see if I was okay. After I told him what had been going on since we had last spoken, I told him I was working overnight again. He asked me whether I was driving back and forth while working overnight. After I told him yes, he told me he wouldn't have that. He told me I could stay with him during the day so I wouldn't have to drive. I was so humbled by his generosity that it almost brought me to tears. We were on a four-days-on, three-days-off schedule, so this would definitely work. I would stay with him for three days and drive home on day four. I gladly accepted his offer and told him if anytime he felt as though I was impeding his space or he wanted me to leave, he should let me know.

This proved to be a game changer. My body felt better because I was able to get more sleep. This enabled me to perform better at night because I was well rested. I was able to make better decisions and focus on the tasks at hand. Another huge game changer for me was that I was partnered with a previous colleague of mine and one of my previous supervisors, Clyde. He had transferred into my facility and was the other overnight assistant manager. This made me feel even more comfortable in my role. He had taught me a lot, so it was fun to see how similar both of our management styles were. Each morning when I got off, I would eat breakfast, watch a movie, fall asleep, wake up around 3:00 p.m., eat dinner, and be at work at 6:00. After my rotation was over, I would drive home to the Gulf Coast with the inevitable task of rebuilding my home on my agenda. This went on for almost a year, and then my time was up as overnight assistant manager. When I arrived at Robert's house the morning after I had worked my last night overnight, I thanked him and told him he had most likely saved my life. If I had driven back and forth an hour after working twelve hours overnight, there was no telling what may have happened. I told him that this would be my final time staying with him, and I would resume driving back and forth because I would be working days. I then handed him an envelope with a large amount of money inside of it to cover any expenses that I may have incurred during my stay. He told me I didn't have to do that but reluctantly accepted and wished me luck.

When my tenure over the dry grocery department and consumables started, I began to get an itch. In almost three years, I had run almost every area in the store. I had gained a ton of knowledge thanks to several great long-term associates. I had learned how to lead as an assistant manager thanks to co-managers Jim and Pat. I was grateful to be assistant manager, but I was eager to become a co-manager as well. After consulting with my supervisors, they agreed that I should begin applying for co-manager positions. They both believed I was ready to take my career to the next level. Some of the other assistant managers did not share the same belief, but that didn't matter to me.

As time went on, I waited for positions to come open that were somewhat drivable so I wouldn't have to move. Nothing came open, so I waited. One day I noticed there was a co-manager spot that came open in McComb. It would be over an hour drive. After careful consideration, I ultimately decided to apply. It was the first co-manager position that I had applied for, so I wasn't expecting much to happen. One day while working, I got a call from a gentleman by the name of James, who told me I should call him Jim. He introduced himself as the store manager and mentioned he was extending me an interview. I gladly accepted and proceeded with the interview. A week passed, and I didn't hear anything, so I assumed I didn't get it. Maybe

I wasn't ready. Maybe I was too young. Maybe it was just a dream and it wasn't my time. I was at the barbershop getting my haircut when I got a call from co-manager Jim. He simply said, "Congratulations, co-manager!" I asked him what he meant. He said, "You got it. I just got a call asking for your release date." A few moments later, I got a call from the McComb store manager. He offered me the job, and I gladly accepted. I was walking around the barbershop in tears and with my hair only half done, filled with joy and a ton of anxiety. I channeled my inner John Cena and shouted inside, *My time is now!*

I finally sat back down and allowed the barber to finish my haircut, but I almost couldn't contain myself. When I got in my car, I called my mother and Keshia to let them know the news. Both of them were excited. When I returned to work, everyone congratulated me but mentioned they were sad to see me go. I told them to never say never, and who knew? I may be back. On my last day, the team gave me a great send-off and wished me luck. When I left that day, I called my mom and told her I was nervous about beginning my new position. She told me to remember what she had taught me. She said, "We don't know what the future holds, but we know who holds the key to the future."

CHAPTER 13

Co-Manager: Act I

Monday morning arrived, and I felt as nervous as one would expect. I also knew I had an hour and fifteen minute drive, which meant I had to get up earlier than usual. As I began my journey down Highway 98, I pondered whether I had made the right decision. I had made a risky choice taking a new position. Instead of waking up an hour before my shift began, I now had to wake up almost three hours before. Instead of getting home in fifteen minutes, I would get home an hour and fifteen minutes later than usual. Instead of being an assistant manager, I was now a supervising assistant manager.

That initial seventy-five-minute drive was the longest drive of my life. When I arrived in my new town, I noticed a vast difference compared to what I was accustomed to. I passed a sign that said the estimated population was thirteen thousand. I also noticed the traffic was much slower than I was accustomed to. I came from a college town, but it was clear to me that this town would be different. When I was a mile out from my new store, I quickly shifted gears and focused on the things that got me to the dance. I said a prayer as I arrived, took a deep breath, and made my way inside my new store.

I put my name badge in my pocket and took a quick walk around. Merchandise and service placement in the store was different, but it was almost the same size as my previous store. I noticed the store was a lot noisier than my previous store.

As I finished up my walkthrough, someone tapped me on the shoulder. It was Jim, the store manager. He shook my hand and told me how excited he was to have me on board. He also told me he remembered me from my first store. He was a co-manager at the time I was an overnight stocker. I was then introduced to the management staff, including the managers I would be supervising. I was also introduced to the other co-manager, Kelvin. Jim informed me that I would be overseeing the general merchandise side of the building, and the other co-manager would be responsible for food. Jim then handed me a set of keys and a radio and wished me luck.

This was my first time as a co-manager, so I knew I would have to rely heavily on Kelvin for guidance during my first few weeks. One of the first things that he taught me was to hold the other managers accountable for their performance. He mentioned that I was not an assistant manager anymore and so I could not operate as such. He then explained to me his daily routine and what needed to be done.

Jim called the morning meeting and introduced me to the store. The associates did not know me or anything about me, so I received a mixed reaction. The majority of the associates stood in silence when I was introduced. I told all of them that I was excited to be part of this team and couldn't wait to get started. After the meeting, I toured the general merchandise backroom. The first thing that I noticed was an endless—and I mean endless—supply of apparel. It was everywhere. Apparel was hanging in the rolling bins, in the layaway bins, and even on the ceiling. There was also apparel in boxes that was not even processed yet. There were pallets of unworked freight from previous nights. There was a ton of backstock from almost every department. I made my way back to the sales floor and toured all my areas alone. I quickly identified the top three areas of concern that needed immediate relief, which included the general merchandise backroom, the garden center patio, and the automotive backroom. I met with the assistant manager over each area to get a sense of how we got here and what we were doing to address it.

The morning flew by, and it was soon lunchtime. Jim took me to lunch and introduced me to a local eatery named the Dinner Bell. It was unique and one of a kind. It had a roundtable style buffet, which was something I was not accustomed to. As we sat there waiting on the food to be served, Jim went over some other basic expectations. He also told me a little about his family and his personal life. He also told me he commuted an hour and fifteen minutes every day. We quickly realized that we had something in common: we lived in the same town. He mentioned we should carpool sometimes, and I told him I couldn't agree more.

We quickly shifted gears back to lunch. He told me it was the best buffet in the South, and if I didn't think so, just wait. The door from the kitchen opened, and a parade of individuals, each with two dishes in hand, made their way out. They had some of the largest bowls I had ever seen. As they placed the food on the table, Jim told me to close my mouth because it was embarrassing. I couldn't help myself. There was mouth-watering fried chicken, greens, mashed potatoes, sweet potatoes, rice, gravy, and virtually anything else that could come to mind. As I began to eat, another lady came out and brought out a serving dish that smelled unbelievable. Jim said that was what they were famous for: eggplants. I tried one, and it was one of the most delicious dishes I had ever had. When we finished eating, I could barely walk back to my car. I told Jim, "Thank you but I am going to have to eat at the Dinner Bell in moderation." After a brief chuckle, we returned to the store.

When we arrived back, Jim continued to establish his expectations through touring. He also gave me background information on the district manager and his team, as well as their expectations. When my shift was over, my body was fatigued and my brain was on overload. Up until this point, I had not realized how much more responsibility a co-manager had compared to an assistant manager. Expectations for me had grown exponentially for me in a matter of ten hours. As I began my journey back home, I second-guessed myself again and wondered whether I made the right decision by accepting the position. That drive was very long and very boring. When I arrived back home, I sat on the couch, and within seconds I was fast asleep. When I woke up, it was time for me to get dressed again and go back to work.

My first day was in the books, and now it was time for day two. As I was driving, I looked down at my fuel gauge and noticed it was almost empty. I had just filled up days ago. I then realized that I was about to incur a very large new monthly expense. At this rate, I would have to fill up my car every two days. The raise that I had just received with my promotion was essentially a wash. It did not matter to me, though, because I knew being a co-manager was not my ultimate goal. Okay, maybe it mattered a little. The drive was very boring. I listened to the same music over and over. It was only day two of driving, and I was losing my mind from boredom.

As my shift began that day, I was greeted by an associate named Lourie. She introduced herself as the accounting associate and gave me some background about her career, including sharing that she had been with the company for over twenty years. She then informed me about a major problem in our accounting office. She told me that she could not get the room to balance, and it was off by several thousand dollars. Now, I had never worked in accounting and always relied on my education and experienced accounting associates in the past to answer any accounting related issues. I was not about to let Lourie know that I could not help her, so I told her I would be up there as soon as I set my bag in the office. When I got to the office, I closed the door, called my previous store, and spoke to the accounting associate. She told me what red flags to look for and gave me troubleshooting techniques that she thought would solve the issue. I went to accounting and tried those techniques, but the room still would not balance. Eventually, after Lourie and I put our heads together, we were able to figure it out.

Later that day, I told Kelvin about my morning and how I almost let it get out that I didn't quite know what I was doing in there today. He reiterated a lesson that my previous co-manager had taught me. He told me that other associates will be the reason that I am successful or unsuccessful. He told me that no one manager knows how to do everything, but I should rely on others to do anything. This was a powerful lesson that I had to be reminded of, and I had to learn to not be embarrassed by that. In order to be successful, I had to develop a successful team. He mentioned that I should rely on good associates like James in sporting goods and Lourie in accounting, adding, "They will be the ones to make you successful."

I got a call from Jim on the radio asking me to come to the office. Sitting there was a gentleman named Mike, who introduced himself as the district manager. Immediately my heart sank. I began to stutter with every question he asked and every statement he made. He told me to grab a pad, and he wanted to walk with me on the general merchandise side of the building. Jim and I met him at the front entrance. He asked me, "What is the first thing you do when you arrive every morning?" I told him that I always drove around the building and the parking lot to make sure we were being a good neighbor. Being a good neighbor involved ensuring that there was no trash or debris visible, along with making sure our landscaping was up to par. It also involved making sure pallets, fixtures, carts, and bales were stacked appropriately. He told me that I was wrong and that was not the first thing I should do. He told me the first thing that I should do was thank God and be grateful that I was a co-manager at only twenty-three years old, because those positions didn't come around every day. He told me there were people twice my age whom he knew and who had been with our company twice as long, and they had not gotten an opportunity like I had. He then told me not to mess it up. I simply replied, "Yes, sir."

He then told me I was correct about being a good neighbor. He then toured my area. We began at the general merchandise entrance and then made our way through pharmacy, cosmetics, health and beauty, and garden center. By the time we got to the garden center, I felt destroyed and utterly defeated. We hadn't even made it a third of the way to the tour, and I already had ten pages of notes. I guess he heard my thoughts, because he repeated to me exactly what I was thinking. He said, "I know it's only your second day, but this is now your area, and two days is long enough to be accountable." We finished up in the garden center and then made our way down hardlines, which included toys, hardware, sporting goods, and automotive. By the time we finished automotive, my store manager's face was as red as I had ever seen it. We then toured homelines, which included housewares, domestics, and stationary. We then finished our sales floor tour in apparel. He walked me toward the men's underwear counter and asked me if I had been over there that day. I told him I had not. He gave me a sarcastic grin and said, "Well, I have." When we rounded the corner and I looked at the counters, I almost passed out. The counters were empty, and the merchandise that was there was not properly zoned for our customers. At that point, Jim excused himself from the tour to go the bathroom. I assumed he left to go throw up from getting sick after looking at my area.

We ended our tour in the backroom, staring at a mountain of unworked and unprocessed freight in the back. He asked me why my area looked like this today. Rather than offer up some excuse that did not matter, I took the high road and took ownership. I told him that I was not pleased with today's tour and that next time he came in, he would see a major difference. He then told me that he would be back Friday, and he expected me to follow through on making a difference. He then left. Feeling humiliated and defeated, I dragged my carcass into the store manager's office and met with Jim. I fully expected Jim to fire me or at least write me up on the spot. He had every right to do so, but he did not. Instead, Jim asked me how I was going to complete all the notes and get my area up to par. I told him my plan, and he told me he expected me to get it done. As I was getting ready to leave the office, Jim asked me to sit back down and close the door. He then told me that some of the assistant managers approached him and told him that they thought I was out of my league. Some of the assistant managers also thought I was too young to hold such a position. He wanted to know whether I could handle managing assistant managers who may have some animosity with me based solely on my age. I told Jim to sit back and watch.

As I drove home that evening, it seemed like the commute was getting longer and longer. I needed to do something to make this drive easier. I spoke to a friend who had a similar commute. He suggested that I get satellite radio, which had sports, comedy, talk, and music rolled up in one. I stopped in Columbia and went to the local supercenter, which was the halfway mark of my daily commute. I went to electronics, purchased a satellite radio, and then drove home. Before I even entered the house, I installed the radio. The service was only twenty-nine dollars a month, but if it made my drive less boring, I was all for it. I left extremely early the next morning knowing I had a long day ahead, but now my commute had become fun. I was able to listen to numerous music channels that had any genre that I wanted. I also was able to listen to sporting events and my personal favorite, comedy. When I was a mile out from the store, I turned off all music and put on my game face. I had to get a lot done in little time, and I had to get it done through people. I drove in the parking lot and, as I was told, thanked God that I was even there as a co-manager. I drove around the building, entered through the garden center, and then immediately began delegating notes.

I had the two general merchandise assistant managers who were there that day meet me so I could cover the notes I needed done. I gave them a time frame for when they needed to be done. I also told them when I would be coming back to check on the notes. I added that I needed their involvement more than ever, and we had a lot to do in a little bit of time. I told them that the district manager was coming back Friday, and we needed to get general merchandise up to standard. I was not going to accept anything less. I told them I would be joining them with delegating these notes because we were going to get them all done today. Both of them were not optimistic about getting ten pages of notes. They voiced their opinion, and I told them that I valued their feedback. I also told them that I was used to executing at a high level, and that was not going to change. I told them I was going to support them, but by the end of the day, we would be done. We all got to work.

When lunchtime came, most of the tasks were already done. I huddled with my team and thanked them for a productive morning, but I also told them that we were not done yet. I also told them, "Don't eat heavy at lunch because if you do, you will be sluggish." So we all went to lunch and then reconvened in the garden center. I noticed that they had done exactly what I had said not to. The assistant managers had gone to a buffet, and now their sense of urgency was gone. They told me they had gone to the Dinner Bell. I immediately knew I was going to have a problem that afternoon getting things done. Needless to say, I had to raise the intensity to accomplish the tasks at hand. Raising the intensity may or may not have involved raising my voice and becoming a tad annoying. By the time 4:00 p.m. arrived, everything was done.

Just as promised, Mike returned a few days later to follow up on his notes and see the progress that we had made. When he finished his tour, he was satisfied with the improvement but challenged me and the store manager to not become stagnant and to continue to push forward. As the months went by, I continued to learn and develop as a co-manager.

November arrived and I was poised to face my biggest challenge yet. It was time for our annual blitz sale. This sale gave customers the opportunity to buy products at unbelievable prices. Electronics, apparel, and toys were usually the most popular categories. Because I was the general merchandise co-manager I was tasked with planning the event. I had to determine how we would prep the product, when we would prep the product, and where we would store it. Then I had to develop a game plan on safely getting it to the sales floor with two thousand people around. Although I already had plenty of experience with this event, this was my first time developing a plan as a co-manager. I wanted to make sure every detail was in place. The annual blitz sale at the time was always held the day after Thanksgiving, so the most challenging part of the plan was how to transition from Thanksgiving to the sale. When the day of Thanksgiving arrived, I had tremendous anxiety. I couldn't sleep the night before because I knew one little hiccup could ruin my entire plan. I had to be at work early to make sure my plan was executed to the letter. I did not get a chance to spend Thanksgiving with my family due to work obligations. Keshia was a little upset at this, but she understood because I had been working retail for a long time.

The sale did not begin until 5:00 a.m. the next day, but I arrived at midnight. We immediately started unloading the storage units and staging merchandise on the floor. Some customers began to dig through the pallets early, so I sent other associates to watch them. By 5:00 a.m., all the merchandise was to the sales floor, all associates were in place, and the sale commenced. All the associates executed their assignments to the letter and worked safe while doing it. My store manager was pleased at the execution. After the sale was over and we cleaned up, I dragged my carcass into my car and drove home. I almost fell asleep several times but was able to make it through. The minute I got home, I went to the bed and passed out. I did not wake up until the next day. My body had been beaten, battered, and abused. I slept almost fourteen hours. I was so glad I was given the weekend off. If I had not had that time, I wouldn't have made it to work the next day. When Monday arrived and I returned to work, the store manager thanked me again for executing a very detailed plan. That was great and all, but it was time for me to get back to learning and growing.

Over the next three years, I had my share of trials and tribulations, including unnecessary inventory growth and turnover. I also had my share of heartbreak. In 2008, I began applying for store manager positions. I spoke with Jim, and he believed that I was ready to lead my own facility. The very first store I applied for was in Pascagoula, Mississippi. The store was huge and was high volume. When I applied, I sent emails to the district leadership to let them know of my interests and my credentials. Several weeks went by, and I hadn't heard anything until one day I got an automatically generated email stating I was not selected for the position. This was tough to hear, especially because I did not receive an interview. I had been told I was good enough, but I couldn't even secure an interview? My store manager at the time told me that they normally did not put co-managers in high-volume stores like that. They would usually move a low-volume store manager into that role, or someone with previous store manager experience.

I couldn't accept that answer, but I understood it. I applied for other stores all over Mississippi, Louisiana, and Alabama. Eventually I did receive a few first interviews, but I never made it to a second interview until Bogalusa, Louisiana, became available. The second interview was in person. When I arrived there, I noticed the store was different. It was two stories and very old. It didn't matter to me—I wanted it! I did everything I could to convince the district manager I was the right fit for the job. It was all for nothing, though, because I was once again not selected for the position. I secured another second interview for a position in Brookhaven, Mississippi. I once again did not get selected for the position. At this point I began to second-guess myself and think I was not good enough.

This continued on until July 2009. I was told something that would alter the course of both my career and personal life. We were informed that instead of two co-managers, there would be four. There would be two co-managers during the day and two overnight. When I heard this, I went into a deep state of depression. One of the perks of becoming co-manager was that I would never have to work overnight, or at least not consistently. On top of working overnight, I had a long commute. By then, we had realigned districts, and my former district manager was back at the helm. He held a meeting with all the store managers and the existing co-managers to give us a snapshot on the new store structure. He then told the co-managers in the room that we would all be going overnight. He mentioned that this was a necessary move to ensure that the store manager would have time to teach and train the new co-manager additions in each store. After he uttered those words, I checked out for the rest of the meeting. I couldn't concentrate or focus. I did not want to go back overnight. I also knew that I had a choice. I could step down from my role and take another position, or I could simply quit and find another job.

I went home that afternoon and just sat back in my recliner, debating my next move. I went in the office room and glanced at the collection of awards and accomplishments that I had set up on my office desk. Did I really want to give up all this? I already knew the answer was no. I didn't work this hard to just give up. I was very driven when it came to achieving goals, so until I became store manager, I couldn't give up. However, I did begin to apply more frequently to open store manager positions. I even went as far as to apply for positions in Florida. I still did not get selected. I met with my store manager and told him I was getting a little frustrated at the selection process. He told me I had all the qualities that a district manager would want in a store manager. He mentioned I was young, hard-working, and motivated, and I knew how to get people behind me. He then got very real with me. He said that although I may have those qualities, there were a lot of managers out there with those same qualities. He also told me there were a lot of associates who had been around for a long time and had paid their dues, and they also wanted a store. He told me to not forget about those store managers who may be in the store manager role but are applying to the stores as well. After thinking back, this made a lot of sense. By then, I had applied for maybe fifteen or so stores, and most of the time another store manager or a very seasoned co-manager ended up getting the job. I may not have agreed with it, but I understood it.

September arrived, and I still had not made store manager, so it was time for me to begin my first rotation overnight. By that point, I had told myself that I was going to push forward and be the best manager that I could be. One perk that I was going to enjoy was the schedule. I would work twelve-hour shifts that rotated four days on and four days off, 8:00 p.m. to 8:00 a.m. Another game changer for me happened when Clyde was selected as one of the co-managers at my store. I had worked with him in other roles in two other stores, so I was stoked when I heard he was coming. I now had someone I could lean on for advice even when things got tough.

When I began my drive to work the first night, I challenged myself to keep getting better, but most importantly, through all the disappointment, I should never give up. I was joined by assistant manager Gail during my rotation. The associates respected her, and she was one of the best in the business. We instantly connected, and our first night was great. We got all the freight worked, the store zoned, and the backrooms spotless. When the store manager came in the next morning, he was impressed with our work. He thanked us and sent us home. I was excited we had a great night, but I was not excited about the long commute I was about to endure after working overnight. I splashed water on my face and began my journey. The first ten minutes of the drive was fine, but after that I lost it. My eyes got heavy, and I began to swerve in and out of lines. If it were not for the pavement improvements outside the white lines that made a sound when I ran over them, I surely would have had an accident. There was a Walmart in Columbia, which was the halfway point between the store and my home. I made it there, pulled in the parking lot, and took a nap. I had no choice. If I did not take that nap, I was going to die or kill someone else. I woke up and continued my journey home. I got off at 8:00 a.m. but did not make it home until 10:00. I went to sleep around noon and woke up at 6:00 p.m. and had to be back at work at 8:00 p.m. I ate, got dressed, and was back on my way again. I did this for four twelve-hour shifts, four days in a row. On the last day, when I got home, I slept all day. My body was worn out. Those four days were a blur, and I had trouble remembering what had happened. Those days off were right on time, and boy, did I need them.

I was overnight for an entire year. Some nights were better than others, but I took all of it as an opportunity to learn, grow, and get better. During that year, I applied for store after store. I didn't get selected time after time. The frustration continued to mount, but I pushed forward.

After my year ended, I was brought back to days. It seemed as though I had spent half of my career overnight as a stocker, support manager, assistant manager, and now co-manager. I was grateful for the experience, but I needed to be on days to spend more time with the store manager and learn. I also needed to talk to the district manager to see what I could do. I did not believe that I was going to be promoted from an overnight co-manager to store manager. Although I was a rising star, I did not want to get lost in the fray. I did everything I could to stand out. I was out and about in the community as much as I could. I became a member of the Lions Club of McComb and a few other civic organizations. I volunteered for

Habitat for Humanity on multiple occasions. I went to other stores when called upon to assist.

In late 2011, I got a call from the district manager stating that there was a store manager who had just gone on a leave of absence, and he wanted to know whether I could run the store while she was out. There was no way I was turning this offer down, especially because I knew it could help get me closer to my goal of actually being the store manager. This would mean that I would be adding an extra twenty minutes to my drive every day, but I didn't care. The store was located in Hazlehurst, Mississippi. I told the district manager I would accept the responsibility. He told me to be there Monday morning at 7:00 a.m. He was going to meet me there to introduce me.

I arrived extremely early that Monday in order to get a feel for the store. I walked around for an hour with no name badge on and developed a mental game plan. Just as promised, the district manager met me there and introduced me to all the associates. He took a quick tour around the store with me and then left. The store had a different layout than what I was accustomed to. It also was a different sales volume than what I was accustomed to. I had to adapt quickly to be successful, and that would start with solving the people puzzle. The store had quite a few outstanding personnel issues that needed to be addressed, ranging from hiring needs to performance issues. Without getting into detail, those issues were solved quickly. Without associates on my side, I knew there was no way I could be effective. I also addressed opportunities with training. Some of the assistant managers told me they needed more training with financials. I did not have the answers to some of the questions that they asked, but I assured them I would find the answers. For the first week, I would go home each night and study the store's profit and loss statement, customer experience dashboards, and several other metrics. Some of them I already knew, and for the ones I didn't know, I taught myself. Another opportunity that needed to be addressed was the availability of products in the store. We had far too many out of stocks and a few broken processes. In order to get this addressed quickly, I took a few basic steps, including establishing great relationships with vendors, secondary suppliers, and our distribution centers. Along with the management staff, we were able to address the broken processes and reestablish broken connections.

During my time there, I was able to reestablish a good relationship with city officials and the community. I was also introduced to some of the best Southern food joints in the state, including a few local eateries. Ever since I was a child, I had always had a thing for Philly steak and cheese sandwiches. One day I was heading to lunch and noticed there was a place called Bumpers right off the highway. I almost had an accident turning in. I had not seen a Bumpers since I had left my hometown for college. I ordered a Philly combo with fries and a vanilla shake. When I bit into the sandwich, all my worries went away, and I felt like a child again. From that day forward, I was at Bumpers every single day ordering a Philly steak. For me, it was almost like an aphrodisiac.

One day I got an email from the district manager to let me know that the store manager was coming back in a week. It had been several months, and needless to say, I was a little heartbroken. The store, the people, and the community had grown on me. On my last day, I was called to the layaway counter to assist a customer. When I arrived, there were over one hundred associates standing there to give me a round of applause and thank me for what I had done for the store. They presented me with a plaque of appreciation and also gave me a few other items to take with me. I almost shed a tear but was able to hold it in. I told the associates to finish what we had started and added that they were in great hands with their current store manager. I left around lunch that day, but before I departed the city, I stopped by Bumpers one last time to enjoy one last Philly Steak and one last vanilla milkshake.

I contacted my store manager to let him know I would be returning next week. He was happy I was coming back, but he also informed me that I would be going back overnight again beginning Monday night. I felt defeated, and it made me a little depressed. I had been overnight for half of my career. I did not complain because I knew this was what I had signed up for, and I knew I had a job to do. I also knew that if I didn't do it, I would probably be fired and never have the opportunity to be store manager. As I began overnight again, I continued to apply for stores. I also continued to get rejection letter after rejection letter. Every night I worked, I would sign on to one of the computers, go to our internal network, and look at the list of store managers under the store alignment lookup hoping to see my name listed one day as a store manager.

In 2012, I had come to a crossroads in my career. I had been driving back and forth for almost six years, and I still had not made store manager. I had done everything I had been asked, and I still hadn't grabbed that brass ring. As I was looking for open store manager positions, I noticed that there was a co-manager position open at my previous store. The position was extremely attractive. If I were to take that position, my drive time would be trimmed down to only ten minutes. The store also had a well-respected store manager at the helm, so I knew I would be going into a great situation. I spoke to my current store manager to seek his opinion about what I should do. He knew of my desire to be a store manager, but he also felt that I needed a change. He knew I was respected by all the associates, and I was his right hand man, but he also knew the other side of the coin.

He understood how I felt every time I told him I didn't get a store, and he wanted what was best for me. He also knew I had gotten so frustrated that I had stopped applying for stores. He told me that I should apply for the co-manager position. I did just that, and a day later, I went through the interview process.

Three weeks went by, and I hadn't heard anything. One night I had just arrived in the parking lot and was driving around the building when my phone rang. On the other end was the human resource manager from the market for which I had applied. By then, districts had been rebranded as markets. She informed me that I had been selected for the co-manager position and would begin at my new-but-old store in two weeks. I thanked her and told her I would not let them down. I took a deep breath to compose myself and debated for a moment whether I had made the right decision. I had come to the conclusion it was the right decision, but it was a painful one. I had been at the store in McComb for six years and had learned a lot. I had the opportunity to work in every store in that market in some form or another. I had been entrusted with being the interim store manager for a store. I was a much better manager than I was when I had first started. I couldn't have asked for a better group of associates. I called Keshia and told her. She was excited that I would be coming off the road and would have more time at home. I then called my mother and could hear the tears flowing from her eyes. She told me that this was what was best for me, and it was also best for her. She told me she was stressed out about me driving home every morning when I got off. I then called Jim and told him. He was excited but not excited. He was happy I had got the position but not happy that he was losing a co-manager he had worked with for six years. Jim and I had developed more than just a working relationship. Jim had become my mentor and more like a father.

The next day, word got out that I had accepted a new position, and the mood in the store drastically changed. It appeared as though everyone in the store was mad at me. I spoke to associates, but they wouldn't speak back. Lourie, one of the associates whom I had developed a great working relationship with, walked by with tears in her eyes, and she couldn't even speak. She told me to give her a minute and walked away. We held the morning meeting behind layaway shortly after. Jim announced that I was leaving, and almost instantly everyone walked away. I said a few words and told everyone that I still had two weeks before I was leaving. No one wanted to hear it. I could see a few people rolling their eyes, and I could see the disgust on their faces.

Around 9:00 a.m. on my last day, I was called into the lounge. As I entered, I couldn't believe my eyes. There had to be three hundred associates in the lounge, greeting me with a round of applause. I was also met with hugs, high-fives, and pats on the back. There was a huge cake with the words "We Will Miss You" written in large letters. Jim led the meeting and told me how much he appreciated me. He told me that he watched me grow from just a co-manager to one of the best in the business. Lourie, Bonita, Katonia, Katoya, Bo-Lee, Evelyn, Roxie, Lisa, Chris, Tabitha, and all the associates and managers shared some kind words and testimonials about the last six years. They presented me with different awards. By now I was in tears and extremely overwhelmed. I told them that this was not goodbye, just "see you later." With tears flowing, I shook every person's hand in that room as they wished me a goodbye. After I packed my car with my belongings and drove away, I took one last look over my shoulder at the store with gratitude and whispered, "Thank you."

CHAPTER 14
Co-Manager: Act II

Monday morning arrived, and it was time for a new chapter in my journey to becoming a store manager. I had an opportunity to show I could be successful in the same role but in a different environment. There were so many possibilities now that I was back home. I had only a ten-minute drive to the store, which meant I would be less fatigued. This meant more energy on the job and the possibility of better decision making. When I walked in the store, there were a few familiar faces still there, including the asset protection associates, department managers, and a few salaried managers I had worked with in the past. I also knew the current store manager. I had worked with the other three comanagers in the past; they all welcomed me back with open arms and told me they were looking forward to working alongside me. Well, that was what two of them said. One of them, Gary, used a little more explicit language when welcoming me back. When I was an assistant manager, Gary took me under his wing and taught me a lot about fresh areas and how to be successful. He had even invited me to his home a few times to meet his family. We had a great relationship.

The store manager informed me that I would be in charge of the general merchandise side during the day. This was music to my ears because I did not want to go overnight again. As I began to take in the new store, I knew that I could not let my eye off the prize. My goal was to become a store manager, and there was nothing that was going to get in my way. I had been co-manager for six years, so I knew I could do the job, but I also knew there were thousands of other managers who wanted the same thing as I did. I had to do something to stand out. I had to do something to separate me from the pack. I didn't quite know what that was yet, but I was going to figure it out. In the meantime, I met the challenges of my new role head-on. Just like my last store, there were a few opportunities surrounding inventory levels and a few other issues that needed correcting. It wasn't easy, but I met those challenges and implemented a plan to get them corrected.

This store was extremely high volume, which meant I had more associates to work with in order to accomplish my tasks. Before I could even think about being a store manager, I had to prove that I was worthy by being successful at my new store, so I approached everything I did with intensity and consistency. I used all the skills that others had taught me, including delegation and empowering people to make decisions. I was able to get associates in my corner by treating them with respect and admiration. That skill was not taught to me by anyone but rather learned over time. As I developed some consistency in my area of responsibility and received great feedback from my store manager, there still was that lingering question that I had yet to answer: What could I do to stand out from everyone else? Although I felt like I was ready to be a store manager, I didn't know whether my store manager or my market manager felt the same way, so I did what anyone in my position would do: I asked them. Both of them felt like I was ready, but they also took the opportunity to give me some valuable feedback about how I could improve in my current role. I took the feedback and immediately implemented it into my routine. Over time, they both noticed the difference and were pleased with my progress.

As I arrived home one day, I was met at the door by Keshia, who said she needed to talk to me. I sat down, and she gave me some news that would change my outlook on life and my career. She told me she was pregnant. We both wept with tears of joy as we embraced. I then looked into her eyes and realized that now everything would be different. Everything I was working for was for our new family. It was no longer about me just becoming a store manager. It was about me giving my child the best life that I could. We did not call our families and decided to keep it a secret until Christmas that year. We purchased some shirts that said "Guess What? I Am Going to Be a Grandparent" on the front. On Christmas Eve, we went over to Keshia's parents' home and gave them each a box to open. When they opened the box and pulled out those shirts, they immediately jumped for joy. They couldn't believe it was true and started calling family members. I asked them not to call my mother because we would tell her tomorrow.

Christmas had arrived, so we met at my mother's home to celebrate the holiday. After some small talk, we handed her a nicely wrapped box. When she pulled out the shirt, she read the front and simply told us, "Thank you for the shirt." After a brief pause, she shouted, "Wait a minute—is it true?" I told her in seven months she would be a grandmother. She wept tears of joy and then called everyone in our family. The first person she called was Aunt Diane to let her know of the good news, and then Aunt Gladys. Both of them came over to the house and congratulated us. As we were driving back to our home, we knew our lives were about to change forever. Keshia told me that she couldn't do this alone, and she needed me to be there for her and the baby. I chuckled and told her that she did not have one thing to worry about. If there was a thing that I wanted more than store manager, it was my own family and being a great dad. She also told me not to give up on my dream of becoming a store manager. She told me to continue to push forward, and she would be right there by my side. I knew at that moment I didn't deserve her. Not everyone would have been so understanding about the long journey of becoming a Walmart store manager. She made me a better person, and now she was about to make me a father.

I am a firm believer that everything happens for a reason. I realized this was the reason I was brought back to a store closer to home. I was brought back home not so I could become store manager but so I could become a dad. My entire outlook on life and my career had changed. I knew now I needed to be home. I knew now that if I was going to attempt to be store manager, my radius now was extremely limited. I was fine with that because nothing was going to stop me from being there for my family. If it took me longer to become a store manager, so be it. Becoming a dad was the most wonderful news I had ever received. I could not wait until I could look into that baby's eyes and tell them daddy was here.

When I returned to work the day after Christmas, everyone noticed I had an extra pep in my step and was laser focused. Finally, during one of the store meetings, I revealed to the associates that I was going to be a dad. Everyone was happy for me and gave me high-fives. When we adjourned the meeting, I saw an associate at one of the back tables with a laptop and several books. She was really getting after it. I could tell she was a student and was on a tight deadline. I walked over to her and asked her what she was studying. She told me she had just enrolled back in college to earn her degree in nursing. She mentioned she was single and had three children. I was in awe. She told me she was working full time, raising three kids, and earning a nursing degree all on her own. She then told me that no one had any excuses when deciding whether to make one's life better, especially if one had a family. It then hit me. I knew how I could stand out and how I could grow as a person as well. I decided at that moment I was going to go back to college to earn my MBA.

Because I was back home and the university was right down the street, it was very doable. There were quite a few classes that were now taught online, so my work schedule would not be a problem. I enrolled that day and was able to begin my classes in January. I knew that pursuing a graduate degree would not guarantee me becoming store manager, but it did guarantee that I would be more attractive to district managers. If I never became a store manager, when I was finished, I would still have earned an MBA that would make me as competitive as ever in the workforce. I had committed to Keshia that I would earn the degree in two years or less, so I got to work. I had been out of college for ten years, so it was a bit of a struggle at first, especially with distance learning.

As I balanced life, work, and college, Keshia's due date rapidly approached. Over the course of the next few months, I was there for every doctor's appointment. I was there for every purchase for the baby. I had assembled the baby crib three months before the baby was to be welcomed into the world. We had decided that we did not want to know the sex of the child and would let it be a surprise when it was born, so everything we brought was neutral.

June finally arrived, and the baby was born. I was the first person the baby saw when it entered the world. The doctor then told us it was a girl, and after wrapping her in a blanket, he handed her to me to hold. When I looked into that little girl's eyes, I told her that my life was now complete, but her life was just getting started. I promised I would be there every step of the way. We decided to name her Kristen.

After two weeks away from work, I finally returned, I had a new outlook on life. I was smiling and calm on the outside, but my adrenaline was at an all-time high on the inside. I had two immediate goals that I needed to achieve. I needed to finish my MBA as quickly as possible to not only enhance my education and skills but also make me more competitive in the highly sought-after store manager field. No one at the store knew I was pursuing another degree, at least to my knowledge. Then I ran into one of the associates I worked with in a campus bookstore. The associate asked me what I was doing there. I was honest and told the associate about my goal. He said he was inspired but also was intrigued, and he wondered how I would balance being a co-manager, getting a graduate degree, and having a new child to take care of. I told him I'd do it by being the hardest worker in the room.

As the months went by, I found myself getting a little burned out. Earning an MBA was a very tough task. Finance, accounting, statistics, and mathematics had all taken a mental toll on me. I was tired physically from the job. I was also tired due to lack of sleep because the baby required a lot of time and, like most newborns, did not like to sleep at night. It didn't matter, though, because being a dad was my greatest accomplishment. Nothing could top being a father to that little girl—until one day something changed. I was called into the office by the store manager. She informed me that I would be going overnight soon. It was time for the other comanagers to come off of nights and rotate to days. This was tough to hear, especially with a new child and pursuing my degree. I thought that maybe going overnight again was a blessing. This meant four nights on, three nights off for my schedule. This also meant that when Keshia went back to work, I could watch the baby during the day until she got off. Also, luckily this transition was happening between semesters, so I could change my course schedule to fit my work schedule.

Several weeks went by. One evening, when the workday was over, I rushed home to speak with Keshia about my schedule. When I walked in, there was a basket full of baby items sitting in the recliner and a poster that read "You are going to be a daddy again!" I couldn't believe it and wept tears of joy. I thought that nothing could top being a dad to one child, but now I was getting the chance to be a dad to two children! We informed our parents that she was expecting again. Needless to say, they were beyond excited. As the months went by, I worked harder on my coursework. I even increased the number of courses I was taking in order to get done faster. This was one of the toughest battles of my life. Similar to when I was getting my undergraduate degree, I would get off work and then go to class. After class, I would spend time with the baby, get a few hours of sleep, wake up and play with the baby some more, and then go to work. I repeated this for several weeks. It came time for Keshia to go back to work, so we decided that I would watch the baby during the day while she was at work, and she would rush home to get her so I could get some sleep before heading to work. It got to the point where my days were a blur, and I couldn't remember them. I would get off, rush to get the baby, and then complete any coursework I had due. The baby would lie in her bed or in my lap while I completed my coursework. If I was typing a paper, she was in my lap, being fed or rocked to sleep. If I needed to go to campus, she would come with me. It got to the point where it became a little unbearable, so I asked for help from my mother and my in-laws. During my four nights I was working, they would help watch the child a day out of the week so I could get some rest. I was extremely grateful for this.

I finished my MBA in August 2014. If no one else was proud of me, I was proud of me. For almost two years, I gave up fun and my personal life in order to achieve my goals not only for me but for my family.

In September, our second child was born. Just like with our first child, we wanted it to be a surprise, so we waited. During delivery, the doctor told us it was a boy. Automatically we knew what that child's name was going to be, and we simultaneously said, "Junior." I had always dreamt of having a son who carried my name, and now that dream was a reality. I looked at my son and told him that my life was now complete for the second time, and I promised to be there for him no matter what. During our stay in the hospital, I sat there holding my son and realized that everything happened for a reason. As much as I wanted to be a store manager, it was not yet time. If I had not taken the co-manager position back home, then most likely there would have not been an MBA, and there may not have been the two most precious children in the world.

I returned to work after two weeks' vacation and began the overnight shift. It was easier this time because I had gotten the graduate degree out of the way. Now more than ever, I needed to become a store manager. I wanted it not only for me but also for my family. I wanted my family to be proud of me, so I started applying again and again. I still did not get selected. My radius was extremely limited now. I had a family, so I could not move across the country at the drop of a dime. I applied for any store manager position that was remotely close and came open.

During this time, I found out that my mother had been diagnosed with cancer for the second time in her life, and she would require surgery and then months of rehab. Although I was worried, I knew my mother was a fighter and that she would make it out of it. I couldn't get it off my mind, though. I could not—would not—lose my mother to cancer. I needed my mother and did not want to live on this Earth without her. Therefore, she did what she does best: she fought. The surgery took a huge toll on her and caused her health to decline even more. She lost weight as she went through chemotherapy. Fortunately, I worked only an hour away, so I was able to drive there and check on her anytime. Sometimes when I called, she would tell me she was all right, but I knew that was not the case. I knew this because I was her son and could always sense when something was wrong. She continued to fight and fight. She was a true inspiration to me because I knew if she could battle through this and win, there was no reason why I couldn't battle through and become a store manager.

November arrived, and I noticed there was a store manager position for a new store in Gulfport that was open. It was not for a supercenter but rather for a Walmart Neighborhood Market. There were two already on the Gulf Coast, so I was familiar with the format. I was also familiar with the format because I had interviewed for both of them and did not get selected. Needless to say, I was intrigued and took some time to apply. This store would be ideal. It was on the Gulf Coast, near my in-laws, and near the beach! I will admit that by this point, I didn't get too excited because I was defeated. I had been a co-manager for eight years and had applied for over forty stores, but I had not been selected.

In early December, I was accompanying my mother to the chemotherapy center for her treatment in Meridian, Mississippi. As I sat in the waiting room, my phone rang. It was the market manager over the Gulfport Neighborhood Market. He told me that he wanted to give me some feedback on my interview. He knew that I had applied for a lot of stores and that he was in my corner, but that unfortunately I was not selected for the position. I wasn't too upset and kind of expected it, so I thanked him for the interview. He then told me he was just playing and that I was selected as the new store manager of Gulfport's very first Walmart Neighborhood Market! I couldn't believe it and started jumping for joy inside the waiting area. I had to step outside because I could not control my excitement. The long nights were worth it, all the sacrifices were worth it, the commutes were worth it, the MBA was worth it, all the sacrifices that I had made and that had led up to this moment were worth it, and I couldn't have been happier. He told me he would hold a conference call later that day to introduce me to the rest of the store managers in his market.

By the time he hung up, my mother was walking out from treatment. She saw the smile on my face and knew something was up. I told her that I had gotten promoted. She was so happy for me but clearly fatigued from the treatment. She told me she never had a doubt. I immediately called Keshia and told her the good news. She screamed for joy over the phone and echoed what she had been telling me all along. She told me the same thing I had told my children when they were born: she would be with me every step of the way.

CHAPTER 15

Store Manager

After I finished the remainder of my time as a co-manager, I prepared for my next chapter. The store that I had been gifted was a brand-new store that was being built. Neighborhood markets were much smaller than supercenters but offered most of the same grocery and consumable products. As my last night approached, I couldn't help but think about all the long nights I had endured, all the long drives, and all the heartbreak that I had experienced from never getting a managing opportunity until now. I also knew I was exactly where I needed to be. It was the right time and the right place. It was my time to shine, and that time started now.

Neighborhood markets were not new to our company. Small-format stores had been around for over a decade but hadn't been a huge priority because our company had focused on our speed engine, the supercenter. With the introduction of more technology, social media, and digital competition, the world of retail was changing. Customers wanted convenience. They wanted somewhere they would be able to quickly get in and get out. They also wanted to be able to get just the essentials. Our traditional big-box brick and mortar stores offered the essentials, but our customers told us they wanted us to do it on a smaller scale. I was excited about the opportunity that was in front of me and knew I was up for the challenge, but before I could offer customers convenience, it was time for me to get to work and understand what neighborhood markets were all about.

In January 2015, I was sent to a small-format academy in Bentonville, Arkansas. The academy was scheduled to last thirty days. This meant thirty days away from my family and away from home. This was the first sacrifice that I had to make in my new role as store manager. My children were small, and I did not want to be away from them or my wife for that long, but I knew I had to do this to get to where I wanted to be. I hadn't worked this hard to become a store manager and then just fail. Keshia was very supportive and again told me not to worry because she was with me every step of the way.

I traveled to Bentonville in style. My company had put me in first class on a Delta flight. I didn't know whether it was a mistake, but I wholeheartedly enjoyed the extra leg room and the around-the-clock beverage service. When I arrived at the airport, I met quite a few other store managers who were there for the small-format academy as well. They were from all parts of the United States, including California, Texas, and Florida. I checked into my hotel and went to my room to be greeted by my new roommate. His story was similar to mine: his store was new, and he was also new to small formats. His store was in Pensacola, Florida. This was exciting news to hear because this meant he was going to be in the same market as me. After a brief conversation, we both turned in for the night. Around 2:00 a.m., I woke up to something or someone cursing me out for no reason. I looked over, and apparently he was having a bad nightmare. It also sounded like the invasion of Normandy. After he fell out of the bed, I chuckled a bit and then went back to sleep.

The next morning, I told him about his night, and he told me he didn't remember any of it. After we laughed, we got dressed, met up with the other store managers downstairs, and drove to the Helen Walton Training Center. Before we got there, we stopped at Dunkin' Donuts for breakfast. This would become our everyday routine during our training. We got to the center early and were greeted by a gentleman named Billy. He shook all our hands and told us he would be our facilitator. After several minutes of small talk, we went into our training room to prepare. For me, this was more than training. This was about my future. Becoming store manager was hard enough, but staying store manager would be even harder. I had to focus and take advantage of all the time that I had there. Bentonville was home to our corporate headquarters and had all the resources I needed to succeed. If I didn't learn it in Bentonville, then I wouldn't learn it. Other store managers poured into the class. There were over forty store managers in my class.

After Billy and the rest of the facilitators introduced themselves, we were given the floor to introduce ourselves and talk about our past experiences and where we were from. I felt a tad intimidated after hearing everyone's story, but there was one thing that we all had in common: the ability to succeed. After introductions, Billy laid out our agenda for the next thirty days. One of the most interesting things I noticed was that we were all assigned a store where we could see how a neighborhood market operated in real time. I learned better by doing, so I was very excited to be afforded that opportunity. Over the course of the next two weeks, I spent time learning and grasping the concept of true leadership and how to operate a new store. We also touched on how to grand open a new store. We were given quite a few contacts that would prove to be very valuable in the future.

We were given weekends off during our training, which allowed us time to explore what Arkansas and the Walmart culture was all about. We spent time at the Five and Dime store and the Walmart museum, which was full of Walmart history. The store even had the original pickup truck that our founder, Sam Walton, had driven. It was truly an eye-opening experience. We also spent time at other key landmarks in Bentonville. During my downtime on weekends, I spent a lot of time at the movie theater, which was located within walking distance of the hotel I stayed at. I don't know what was going on that month, but there were no good movies in the theater. Some of the movies were so bad that they should have gone straight to home video. The only movie that I found interesting was *Interstellar*. I saw *Interstellar* at least five times when I was training. For a moment, I felt like I was the star of the movie. I thought I was Matthew McConaughey because I had seen it so much. The last time I saw it, I was the only one in the auditorium, and I could almost repeat every word of that movie.

Staying in Arkansas was challenging because I was away from my family. I had become friends with some of the other store managers, but it still wasn't the same. My roommate and I grew close knowing that we would be working together in the same market in the future. Our last day of training had arrived, and I felt like I had all the information I needed to be successful and hit the ground running. Billy and the rest of the facilitators gave us all a completion certificate during a nice graduation ceremony. Armed with a ton of knowledge, and more importantly a lot of notes, I exchanged pleasantries with the other store managers and then headed to the airport and flew home. I was grateful for what I had learned but even more grateful to see my family.

When I arrived back, I was contacted by the market manager, who told me to be in Mobile, Alabama, on Monday morning to assist at another store. He also told me that my roommate, Frank, would be joining me. When we arrived at that store, a heavy dose of reality sank in. The store was relatively new, so there were quite a few growing pains surrounding their processes. During my time there, I learned how to troubleshoot issues with strategic decision making. I also relearned how to work freight and get it on the shelves. I spent a lot of time doing that to help them get caught back up. We found this barbecue joint near the store that may have been the best barbecue on the planet. It also could have been that we were very hungry as well. Regardless, it was great and gave us the energy we needed to finish the day.

I had the opportunity to meet the regional manager while I was at the store. I learned quite a few lessons from him during his visits to the store. We stayed at that store for a few weeks while our stores continued to be built. One day while I was stocking freight, I got a call from a lady named Diane. She told me she would be working with me to secure a location for my hiring site, and she would need me near my store on Monday to view some sites. I almost hated to leave Mobile because of that delicious barbeque, but I had no choice. Diane contacted me Monday morning and gave me a few sites to view. Some were better than others, but one stood out from the rest. It was behind the Walmart Supercenter. The site was relatively new and had over 5,500 feet of office space. All the rooms were divided and would allow for privacy while conducting interviews and other business. I contacted Diane and told her I did not have to look anywhere else; that was where I wanted to set up my hiring center. She told me she would begin working on it right away.

My next step was to hire a personnel manager. I had already been contacted by several associates from different stores inquiring about the role, so I was excited to know I had a solid applicant pool.

While my hiring center lease was being finalized, I was assigned to both the D'Iberville Neighborhood Market and the Biloxi Keesler Neighborhood Market as my new base of operations for now. It was in D'Iberville where I would meet another very influential associate in my career. He was the store manager and had a wealth of knowledge and experience after having been with the company for over thirty years. He welcomed me to his store and to the market with open arms. The store manager of the Biloxi Keesler Neighborhood Market welcomed me with open arms as well. She told me if I needed anything, she would do what she could to give me all the guidance I needed to be successful.

I was driving to D'Iberville for my first day at my new base of operations when Diane called and told me that she had secured my site, but I had to go sign the lease that morning. I turned around and did just that. The realtor shook hands, handed me the keys, and wished me luck. I stood in the middle of the hiring site alone. As I took a deep breath and looked around, a little voice whispered to me, "Time to go to work." There was a large meeting table in one of the rooms, so I decided that I wasn't going to D'Iberville. I was going to stay and get started. I gathered a few things from my car, sat at the table, and began going over my notes from small-format academy. I then began placing phone calls and conducting interviews for the personnel manager role at my facility. There were several great candidates, but one candidate stood out above the rest. She had a great interview, and I could tell she had a wealth of experience. She had been with the company over twenty years and had served in multiple roles throughout her tenure. She also had worked with my market manager in the past when he was a store manager. I took some time to make a final decision, but ultimately Stacy was my top pick.

Instead of going back to D'Iberville or Biloxi, I took some time over the next few days in the hiring center placing phone calls to get the ball rolling on systems being set up and other important business, including selecting candidates to interview for assistant manager positions. I also spent time conducting interviews for assistant manager positions. I had several great candidates who had applied, and I was eager to make my selections. During this time, I received a call from a lady named Bridget. She was the lead store planner assigned by our home office to get my hiring center up and running, and she was also responsible for ensuring the store was set up properly. She gave me details on when my systems would arrive and which member of her store planning team would be assisting with installation. Before that happened, it was decision time for me. The very first person I hired was Stacy. When I called and offered her the job, I could tell she was filled with joy, and she told me she wouldn't let me down. After I hung up, I was eager to meet her in person, so the following day I drove to her current store in Wiggins to introduce myself. The first thing that I noticed about her was her outgoing personality and the energy she was about to bring to our new store. I also took some time to speak to her store manager and let him know I had selected her. I could tell he was happy for her but was disappointed that she was leaving his store. That disappointment gave me the reassurance I needed that I had made the right decision. I informed my market manager that I had selected Stacy, and he told me I couldn't have made a better decision.

Over the next week, I finalized my assistant manager selections. I was allowed to have four managers, including two overnight assistant managers, a fresh manager, and a food and consumables manager. Because this was a new store, I knew I needed experience. My wish list included three assistant managers currently in the role and one assistant manager trainee. However, I knew that this might not be feasible after multiple rounds of interviews with different candidates from the Gulf Coast. I therefore made my final selections. For my first three selections, I chose an existing assistant manager from the D'Iberville Supercenter, an hourly supervisor from the Pass Christian Supercenter, and an hourly supervisor from the Gulfport Supercenter. My final selection was an assistant manager from the D'Iberville Neighborhood Market who came highly recommended from the market manager. After partnering with the market health and wellness manager, I now had a new pharmacy manager as well. Pharmacy was one of the most important parts of a neighborhood market, if not the most important. Now that I had my core leadership in place, the time came to get the hiring center up and running. Stacy's current store manager was gracious enough to release her within a week of her selection. When she arrived at the hiring facility, she told me how excited she was to take on the role of personnel manager at our new store.

Our hiring site's systems had already arrived, so all we had to do was get set up to begin hiring. Chris from store planning arrived to begin our initial systems setup. It took us all day to finally get set up, but we still could not get our systems online. We reconvened the next day and continued on. While Chris worked on systems, Stacy took the time to put her special touch on our new base of operations. She purchased some nice décor and other items to make our center truly inviting. We also had a few hiring banners made to place in front of the store to let people know we were hiring. After two days of rigorous running, we were online and ready to go. Chris left on that Tuesday and told us if we needed anything, we should let him know. Stacy spent the next three days making sure our hiring site was almost flawless. I spent the next few days setting up meetings and making sure that every box on my checklist was checked off. I scheduled my first management meeting for the following Saturday. By then I had already met all the managers in person, but I wanted to bring them together as a group to establish a few expectations. Saturday arrived, and we all met at the hiring site. I let them all know that we would be open for business on Monday and would immediately begin hiring for all positions. All the managers were very excited and were ready to go. I gave them their schedule for the week and told them that I would see them on Monday. After the managers left, Stacy opened up electronic requisitions for all the different positions we had available. We had already gotten multiple inquiries from both internal and external applicants so I knew we would have no trouble filling each position.

Monday morning arrived, and all the managers really got after it. They spent countless hours on the phone setting up interviews. We also were able to conduct several interviews on the spot as individuals came to apply in person. There were a few setbacks, including individuals who accepted positions but then declined. Stacy was having orientation two to three times each week. We had only so many computers that associates could use, so she did her best to keep all the orientations staggered. This continued on for weeks until we had every position filled. I was excited about what we had accomplished in such a short period of time, but I was also excited about the quality of people that we had hired. We had a good solid mix of transfer associates from other facilities along with new external associates. I also had a good mix of experience, including several long-term associates. I felt good about our core group of supervisors and some of our external hires who would eventually become supervisors. I also felt really good about our primary accounting associate. He had a wealth of knowledge and had been with our company for several years already. He had a college education and knew finance, so I considered myself lucky to have found someone with prior experience in accounting. I felt great about my primary backroom receiving associate. She came highly recommended and had over twenty years of experience working for our company. She would be responsible for checking in all vendors and receiving our merchandise off of trucks, so she had one of the most important jobs in the store.

During our time in the hiring center, I would often meet with my management staff. We would have ongoing discussions about how they would be successful in their areas. All of us, including me, had worked at a Walmart Supercenter at one time or another, so we had plenty of experience. In fact, we had so much experience that I made a bold statement I had to deliver on. I said, "It is a Walmart Neighborhood Market—how hard could it be?" As the store came together, I continued to grow confident. At least once or twice a week, my leadership team and I would tour the facility, and I would report the progress to the market manager. The store was beautiful. All the cases were brand-new, the floors were shining, and the new LED lighting had the store shining bright. It was truly a magnificent sight. As the contractors continued on, we sent our associates to other stores to train. We sent some of them to the D'Iberville Neighborhood Market, and some went to Biloxi. Two of the assistant managers had to attend management training for several weeks, so I was without them for a while. When they returned, it was time for us to transition from the hiring center to the store. We announced the move to all our associates and gave them all a schedule regarding when to report to our new store. It took us a week to transition all the systems and all the equipment from the hiring center. On Friday, the entire store planning team arrived to assist us with the move. By Friday afternoon, we had thoroughly cleaned the hiring site and had it ready for the next tenant. After everyone left, I met the landlord so we could walk and do a final inspection alone. We passed with flying colors, so I handed him the keys, thanked him, and then left for the weekend.

Monday morning arrived, and I was eager to get started. I met the store planners at the store early so they could brief me on how we would get the store set up while working around the contractors. After we went over our game plan, we patiently waited for all our associates to arrive. All of them had been at other stores training, so this was the first time that the management staff would have a chance to work with them hands-on. After everyone arrived, I had my very first store meeting. It was a chance for me to set the tone with my team for the very first time. I ended the meeting with a powerful Walmart cheer so loud that the neighbors could hear.

Over the next four weeks, we spent time building counters, unloading trucks, stocking, zoning, scrubbing, cleaning, and most importantly learning. The management staff learned about their associates, and the associates learned about them. Managers learned associates' strengths and opportunities. They learned more of what I expected as store manager as well. I learned what both my company and my market manager expected of me. We were also preparing for our grand opening. I had no doubt that the store was going to be successful. We were in the second largest city in the state, and the store was built right off the busiest highway in the city. One of the assistant managers was in charge of putting together everything for our grand opening, including securing keynote speakers. During my time at the small-format academy in Arkansas, I took pages of notes about how a grand opening ceremony should go. My roommate from the academy, Frank, was set to open his store a week earlier than mine, so I told the assistant that we would attend his grand opening ceremony to get ideas on how ours could be successful. After his ceremony, we coupled what guidelines we had and what we had planned with his and made it our own. It was a week out from our grand opening, and we were very excited for our opening.

After months of traveling, training, hiring, and learning, the store was ready to go. The store was clean, well stocked, zoned, and most of all new. Two nights before we were set to open, we hosted a fun night for all the associates and their families. We had refreshments and even a live band. There was so much excitement in the air that I almost couldn't contain myself. After family night was over, we spent the next two days making sure the store was perfect. Then it was time. June 10, 2015, had arrived, and it was time for me to open my very first store as the very first store manager. The ceremony was filled with glamour from top to bottom. Both local news stations were there. There was also a who's who set of city officials who attended, including several councilmen and the superintendent of education. He brought thirty kids with him to help him with the Pledge of Allegiance. It was an awesome sight. We also presented several thousand dollars' worth of grant checks to local schools and food banks. When we were getting ready to close the ceremony, I asked one of our store planners to lead us in a Walmart cheer. Jason was a former drill sergeant in the military, and boy, did it come out of him during that cheer. His neck had so many veins popping out of it that I thought I was going to have to call the paramedics, who were already on site. He delivered the most intense and aggressive Walmart cheer I had ever heard. It was so thunderous that the ground shook. After everyone's blood pressure came back down from his cheer, the chamber of commerce came up to hold our ribbon-cutting ceremony. They handed me the scissors to cut the ribbon. As I was about to cut, I stopped and asked my very first associate to come up and do the honors. Stacy was very surprised and somewhat embarrassed that I asked her to do it. She giggled and blushed as she cut the ribbon, and she welcomed everyone to our new store!

After all the glitz and glamour, and after all the dust settled, it was time for me to get to work as the store manager. Over the next year, I found out I was wrong about a few things. First, I thought becoming a store manager was the hard part. *Staying* in the role of store manager was the hard part. The store had exceeded all financial expectations and was the highest volume store in the company at the time. This also meant added stress for which I was not prepared. I was not prepared mentally or physically for the grind of running a high-volume neighborhood market. I thought that my store would be like the other stores in which I had trained. Those stores received merchandise trucks only a few times a week and were low- to medium-volume stores. I should have known better. There were times I didn't have enough staffing due to call-outs. I experienced unexpected turnover with my management staff along with quite a few hourly associates. There were times where we were backed up with freight in the backroom, and I didn't know how to dig my way out of it. This caused sales to suffer, and it also caused unneeded stress on all the associates. There were days that the market manager would come in and chew me out because of store conditions. There were also days I could see in his eyes that he wanted to get rid of me and did not believe I could be successful. There were days I would go home and almost collapse upon arrival. Keshia would always ask how my day was, but I would get off the subject and try to redirect the conversation to something more positive.

During that first year, I was under more stress than I could have ever imagined. I never considered quitting, though; I wasn't built that way. I had dealt with tremendous adversity all my life, and I knew I had to make some changes in order to be successful. I had an advantage over everyone else by being the hardest worker in the room, so I knew I had to be that person yet again. In early February 2016, we had our year-beginning meeting in Denver, Colorado. This meeting gave us the opportunity to meet with senior leadership and all store managers in the company to discuss the upcoming year and establish clear expectations about how we would be successful going forward. It was held at the Denver Convention Center, which was located downtown. As we were transitioning between sessions, I walked alongside the store manager from D'Iberville, discussing business. I went to step down a flight of stairs but tumbled and fell to the floor. I immediately heard a pop in my shoulder and knew something was wrong. This was the most embarrassing moment of my life. There had to be at least two thousand store managers surrounding me and asking whether I was okay. An asset protection representative arrived and escorted me to a room to be examined, where they informed me I had dislocated my shoulder. I was hauled off in an ambulance to a local medical center. Frank rode in the ambulance with me as I writhed in pain. After I returned to the hotel, I was met with a few concerns but mostly laughter and jeers. I told all of them that I was embarrassed more than anything. I also told them to wait until this time next year, and I assured them that I was going to make up for this gaffe.

After the meeting, on the flight back home, I couldn't help but continuously pound my fist against the seat in front of me. I had been embarrassed and humiliated due to an unforeseen circumstance. After I got over it, I began recapping what I had learned from the meeting and how I could deliver the message to my team. One part of that message that our CEO spoke about was being the best store in town. This portion of the message resonated with me at an unbelievable level. There was a ton of competition on the Gulf Coast, including another store like mine. How could I make our store the best store in town? The short answer was I couldn't. I couldn't do anything—but *we* could. If I could make my team the best in town, then everything else would follow suit. That was exactly what I did.

Over the course of the next year, I spent almost every day at the store teaching, training, and holding people accountable. I spent so much time at the store that the associates started asking me to go home. Even on my days off, I would come in to see how things were going. I also came in at night to see the overnight crew. The entire year was full of growing pains and opportunities, but it was also full of wins. The management staff and the associates were better than ever. Through many minor additions and subtractions, I truly believed we had the best team in the business. During that year, we also added a few extra services, including online grocery pickup, which proved to be a game changer. During the same year, stores were realigned, which meant that I would be under the leadership of a new market manager, who would push me to my limits. On January 27, 2017, we opened a new, state-of-the-art fuel station, which was a great addition to our store. We had all the convenience that any customer could want. Customers could shop in-store or online. They did not have to come in for their prescriptions and could instead use our drive-through pharmacy, and they could get fuel all at Gulfport's very first Walmart Neighborhood Market. By the end of that year, the store was at full throttle and firing on all cylinders. Sales and profit had exceeded all expectations, we had a great annual inventory, our customer service metrics were higher than they had ever been, and the associates were more engaged than ever.

February 2017 arrived, and it was now time for our annual year-beginning meeting. I always looked forward to these because it gave me a chance to learn and a chance to meet with my peers. The meeting was held in Orlando, Florida, and was as extravagant as they come. The meeting was designed for our company to showcase new products as well as any upcoming initiatives. The meeting was also designed to recognize outstanding performance by managers across the company.

Our first session served as a kickoff and to get us fired up about the year ahead of us. As I sat there and diligently took notes, I thought about my store, what we had accomplished this past year, and how we could build on it and keep the momentum going. After an hour, we transitioned to our breakout sessions. Neighborhood markets and supercenters had their own separate sessions. After a few introductions, we moved into the recognition portion of the session. First, associates who had reached service milestones were recognized, including an associate who had been with the company for over thirty-five years. Next, several store managers were recognized for exceptional operational performance metrics. After this, it was time for Store of the Year presentations. There were five regions in neighborhood markets, and one by one, the regional managers presented the award for their region. When it was time for our market's region, I began to wonder whether I had a shot. I had had a great year the previous year, but I also knew there were a lot of other stores that had great years, including some in my market. The regional general manager approached the stage with a certain swagger that could not be duplicated. He had toured my store numerous times the previous year, so I was very familiar with him. He thanked everyone for their hard work and dedication and then talked about his store of the year. He said some things and quoted a few metrics that sounded familiar to my store. Toward the end of his speech, I was sure my heart was racing four times its normal pace. He then said, "My regional store of the year is ..." After a brief pause that seemed like an eternity, my store number appeared on the large screen on the stage. At that moment, it seemed like time stood still. For about five seconds, as other managers gave me a round of applause, I sat in my chair and couldn't move. Finally, one of the other managers tapped me and told me to go up on stage. As I made my way on stage, all I could think about was the individuals who had helped me get to this point, including past and current associates, managers, and my current market manager. As I humbly accepted the award for regional store of the year, I was informed that I now would be competing for store of the year for the entire company.

I sat back down and was greeted with a hug from my market manager to let me know how proud he was of me. He also whispered in my ear that he truly believed I was not done yet. He told me I was going to win for the entire company tomorrow. I told him I appreciated the confidence, but I didn't have a shot. He then said, "You didn't think you had a shot at the regional store of the year either." I did not hear anything the other presenters said for the rest of that session. I spent time internally basking in the glory that came with a regional store of the year win. I also spent time texting my management staff to let them know of our win. They were all excited. When the meeting concluded, I got down on my knees and thanked God for this win because I knew without him, it wouldn't have been possible.

The next day arrived, and all I could think of was the possibility of winning. What if I did win store of the year for the company? I was just a kid from a small town in the heart of Mississippi who grew up in a loving but challenging environment. Was I about to achieve the impossible? During the last general session of the meeting, all regional stores of the year winners were invited to sit near the stage so the overall winner could walk up and be recognized. After our senior leadership gave their closing speeches, they moved into the final recognition portion of the meeting. They recognized other managers for company achievements, and then the time came for our executive vice president and our CEO to recognize the store of the year recipient for the company for neighborhood markets. All five regional store of the year winners were placed on a large screen for all to see. The executive vice president congratulated us all and then mentioned there was one that stood out above the rest. She then began reading a few operational metrics that sounded familiar. I went into a proverbial metamorphosis as my soul floated from my body. When she mentioned that this store had the highest number of online grocery orders of any store in the company, I knew I had won. A few seconds later, my name and store number appeared on the large screen as she called my name as the 2016 Store of the Year award winner!

As the lights dimmed and a video package about my store played on the big screen, I had to wipe away tears as I was escorted to the stage by one of the hosts. When the lights came back on, I was handed a four-foot plaque recognizing my store as the store of the year. I was congratulated by the executive vice president and the CEO and then turned around for a brief photo op. All I could think while I held that plaque was, *Don't fall!* I was given one last round of applause from my peers, and then I turned around and was escorted off the stage and back to my seat. As I sat there and gathered my composure, a wave of thoughts and emotions began to flow. I started thinking that everything I had been through was worth it and had brought me to that point. The long nights, the long commutes, and all the failures had brought me to this point. The heartbreak of being turned down forty times for various store manager positions I had applied for had somehow driven me to this moment. Maybe I wasn't ready to run a store earlier in my career, and the individuals who had turned me down had done me a favor. If I had gotten selected for any other store, I may have not been successful. I was selected at the right place, the right time, and more importantly by the right person.

When I finally came back down to Earth, I checked my phone. I had received a flood of text messages, calls, and emails congratulating me on the award. Apparently word had already gotten back to my family and other key members of the community before I left the stage, because they all reached out. I even got texts from members of my Rotary Club. I thanked them but told them I didn't do it alone. There should have been a hundred chairs on that stage for all the store associates to accept the award with me, because they had earned it. We had earned it. When the session ended, I rushed to grab my luggage and then proceeded to one of the charter buses for the airport. On the flight back, I couldn't wipe the smile off my face. My store was the 2016 store of the year!

When I got back to my store, I told all the associates how proud they should be and how proud I was of them. What an accomplishment! A few days later, I was sitting in my office, doing some work and preparing for my store's next chapter. I looked down at the phone and thought back to when I was a stocker and had sat in my first store manager's office and decided what I wanted to do. Looking at that phone reminded me of what I saw in his office. It had come full circle. As I sat there, someone told me on the walkie-talkie that I had a phone call from our COO, who wanted to again offer congratulations. With as much pride as I could muster, I told them to transfer it to my office. "Transfer the call to the store manager's office, extension 170."

APPENDIX:
ACHIEVING YOUR GOALS

1. Put God first in all that you do. There were plenty of days and nights that I wanted to give up and give in. There were plenty of days that I began to question him out of frustration. God has a plan for all of us, and we must be patient until the plan is complete. Talk to God and let him know that you need his help. Don't be afraid to pray. Prayer changes things!

2. In order to achieve your goals, first develop your goals using the SMART method. Goals should be specific, measurable, attainable, realistic, and timely. When you achieve a goal, replace that goal with a new one. Your goals should always continue to evolve.

3. In order to achieve your goals, become the hardest worker in the room. There are those who may have financial and social privilege. There are those who may have been given more than you or who know more people than you, but it does not matter! When I was in high school, I remember a few football players who did not get much playing time. I would hear a few of them say it was all politics, and the players whose parents gave a lot of money to the booster club got more playing time. I did not realize until now what lesson was being taught during those moments.

Coaches get paid to win. Coaches are going to put the players in the game that give them the best opportunity to win. If you want to play, work harder! I believe this in sports, and I believe it in life. It does not matter where you come from or what your background is. Stay the course and work harder than everyone else. Get up early and stay up late. You will have plenty of time for sleep after you reach your goal. Do what you have to do to get to where you want to be!

4. In order to achieve your goals, you must mentally prepare yourself. You must focus like never before. If something in your life is hindering you from achieving your goals, remove it.

5. In order to achieve your goals, you must find someone to help you along the way. You must have a support system. This could be a spouse, a relative, a friend, or a colleague from work. You need feedback!

6. In order to achieve your goals, you must continue to learn and get an education. Never stop learning! This does not necessarily mean going back to school to earn a degree. It means interacting with an experienced educator or an experienced manager as a learning opportunity. It means using experiential learning as a means to grow. Use the art of self-management as a key component on your journey to achieving your goals. Don't wait on someone to teach you—go and get it.

7. In order to achieve your goals, you must start by addressing the person in the mirror. Maybe the way you have been doing things at your job has been wrong all along. Maybe you have gotten defensive and not adhered to the feedback you have been given from your supervisor. Maybe you have not gotten any feedback at all. In order to unlock your full potential, start by looking at and fixing the person in the mirror.

8. In order to achieve your goals, you cannot expect to achieve them overnight. Sometimes longevity is the key to success. Just because you didn't get that promotion doesn't mean you should walk away. It means that it wasn't meant for you, and you should keep fighting. Until you reach your goal, continue to do your absolute best in everything you do.

9. In order to achieve your goals, you must be at your best during your darkest moments. No matter who you are or where you come from, there will be dark moments. You must rise to the occasion and refocus yourself. You must get up and fight! During your darkest moments, look within, dig deep, and make those dark moments turn into light. There is no greater teacher than making mistakes. It was not during my winning moments that I learned. I learned by losing in both my profession and personal life. Learn from your mistakes and then teach someone else not to make those same mistakes.

10. In order to achieve your goals, you must stay the course and never give up. Do not quit, and do not give in. When you want to quit, talk to your support system. When you want to quit, continue on your journey anyway! Be prepared to get tuned down forty times just to get one yes!

ACKNOWLEDGMENTS

I would like to give thanks to God for giving me the energy and the humility to write my story. Without your mercy, I would not be here. Thank you for giving me justice when I deserved it, and thank you for giving me grace when I didn't deserve it. I would like to give a special thanks to my children Kristen and Kevin Jr. I love you with every ounce of my soul. I would like to thank my mother, JoAnn Gaines, for being the best mother I could ask for. It is because of your sacrifice that I became the man I am today, and for that I am forever grateful. I thank you for always encouraging me and always being there for me during my darkest hours. I would also like to thank my aunt, the late Diane Everett, who was an accomplished author. Thank you for serving as an inspiration to pen this novel. I would like to thank my other aunt, the late Gladys Spencer, who always wanted the best for me. I would also like to give thanks to my entire family, who always supported me over the years.

Thanks to all my friends for your unwavering support over the years. Thanks to all my teachers who encouraged me to be the best I can be. A special thanks to my sixth grade teacher, Carol Taylor, who once told me that I should be a writer. Thank you to all my coaches who challenged and pushed me beyond my limits, including Principal Robert Hawthorne and Coach Johnny Gray. Thank you to all my professors at the University of Southern Mississippi who would not let me fail. Lastly, with every ounce of humility in my soul, thank you to every work colleague who has been instrumental in my career journey. Without all of you, none of this would have been possible!

Printed in the United States
By Bookmasters